Training for
Both Ends
of the Leash

AVERY

A MEMBER OF PENGUIN GROUP (USA) INC.

NEW YORK

Training for Both Ends of the Leash

A GUIDE TO COOPERATION TRAINING FOR YOU AND YOUR DOG

KATE PERRY

and YVONNE CONZA

Published by the Penguin Group
Penguin Group (USA) Inc., 375 Hudson Street, New York, New York 10014, USA • Penguin Group (Canada),
90 Eglinton Avenue East, Suite 700, Toronto, Ontario M4P 2Y3, Canada (a division of Pearson Penguin Canada Inc.) •
Penguin Books Ltd, 80 Strand, London WC2R 0RL, England • Penguin Ireland, 25 St Stephen's Green,
Dublin 2, Ireland (a division of Penguin Books Ltd) • Penguin Group (Australia), 250 Camberwell Road,
Camberwell, Victoria 3124, Australia (a division of Pearson Australia Group Pty Ltd) • Penguin Books
India Pvt Ltd, 11 Community Centre, Panchsheel Park, New Delhi–110 017, India • Penguin Group (NZ),
67 Apollo Drive, Rosedale, North Shore 0632, New Zealand (a division of Pearson New Zealand Ltd) •
Penguin Books (South Africa) (Pty) Ltd, 24 Sturdee Avenue, Rosebank, Johannesburg 2196, South Africa

Penguin Books Ltd, Registered Offices: 80 Strand, London WC2R 0RL, England

Most Avery books are available at special quantity discounts for bulk purchase for sales promotions, premiums,
fund-raising, and educational needs. Special books or book excerpts also can be created to fit specific needs.
For details, write Penguin Group (USA) Inc. Special Markets, 375 Hudson Street, New York, NY 10014.

ISBN 978-1-58333-451-5

Printed in the United States of America
3   5   7   9   10   8   6   4   2

Book design by Meighan Cavanaugh

While the authors have made every effort to provide accurate telephone numbers, Internet addresses, and other contact
information at the time of publication, neither the publisher nor the authors assume any responsibility for errors,
or for changes that occur after publication. Further, the publisher does not have any control over
and does not assume any responsibility for author or third-party websites or their content.

CONTENTS

ONE-LESS-DOG MANTRA

Every household is different, and so is every dog. Taking a personal interest in each one of my clients' cases has provided me with the opportunity to achieve my "one-less-dog" mantra. Building and enhancing the bond between owners and dogs in fun and innovative ways means one less dog is sent to a shelter and one less dog is euthanized.

The one-less-dog mantra is what led me to write this book. It's my giveback to the dogs that have rewarded me and enriched my life. My intention is for prospective and current owners, whether adopting, rescuing or purchasing a dog, to have a comprehensive, user-friendly read that supports the training process.

INTRODUCTION

Who I am as a trainer has a great deal to do with Sophie, my re-homed pug. She entered my life at a crucial time. Jane, Sophie's previous owner, was diagnosed with colon cancer. As her illness progressed, Sophie became more accustomed to spending her days by Jane's side. When Jane was hospitalized for three weeks, I became a beloved auntie to Sophie.

Sophie stayed at my home, which is where I first became aware of her separation anxiety. I took her to my classes in part to manage her anxiety and in part to train her. When Jane returned home, it was to settle her affairs. Sophie's welfare was her biggest worry. How should she go about the process of re-homing her dog?

During those three weeks, I had time to think about the situation and bond with Sophie. This was a dog with behavior challenges that needed to be addressed. This was a dog that loved, but was losing, her owner. This was a dog that was small in size but huge in spirit. I had fallen for

Queen Sophie, a non-wallflower lady with a Bea Arthur "Maude" shoot-from-the-hip character.

I told Jane I'd take her dog if she gave me her blessing. The image of Sophie snuggling up to Jane as the final decision was made remains unforgettable for me. There was a calmness in the dog that I hadn't seen before. Two souls were communicating what needed to be said. That evening I packed Sophie's things and snapped on her leash. We said good night, realizing that it might be good-bye. The next day Jane died.

PROFESSOR SOPHIE

I started bringing Sophie to my classes because of her separation anxiety. As time progressed, she assumed the dog-on-dog instructor role of doling out decisive discipline, not aggression, to the pups as needed. She was first a student and then became a teacher. Professor Sophie's lively and entertaining lessons imparted proper and useful cut-off signals for the pups. When they pounced in her face, she gave a shoulder slam, letting them know to respect their elders. If they became increasingly disrespectful and tried to bully her, she pinned them down with controlled force, not hurting them, but getting them to rethink their actions with her and other dogs. When they jumped repeatedly on her back, she responded with a high-pitched bark-bark in their faces. *"Wanna play with me? Play nice."*

My velvet black pug taught me to look more closely at interactions between dogs, among dogs and people, and with dogs and their environment. She made me realize that the answers are usually right in front of us. Sophie's "show and tell" demonstrations with puppies paralleled my training techniques with owners. Teaching put Sophie to work and served as an innovative stress reliever that reduced her separation anxiety. Her coping skills were advanced and her confidence boosted.

Professor Sophie's empowering turnaround reaffirms to me that cooperative behavior is a strategy that balances connection, willingness and motivation. While dogs speak a different language than us, we share a common desire for a social partnering that stabilizes our lives. Sophie and I continue to grow together as educators: I teach the owners and she trains the puppies.

Observing dog-on-dog interplay clued me in to the importance of setting a dog up for success. Professor Sophie's techniques and style focus on this. Corrections and redirects are done in such a way that her students begin offering their teacher good behavior. They look for the rewards attached to doing what is not only acceptable but also desired behavior. The environment includes play and an understanding of social ranking. Sophie is the top dog who leaves it to the students to work out social positioning among themselves, though she steps in when needed.

I've always understood the canine thinking and behavior principles that Sophie demonstrates in class. However, it wasn't until she became my dog that scientific theory validated real-life experience. Along with my extensive training sessions with over two thousand dogs, and ongoing studies in the art and science of professional dog training, her symposiums are now forever integrated with me.

Sophie taught and inspired me to look at dogs not just with my eyes, but also through hers. That's when I began to understand how training techniques could become more user-friendly and innovative. No longer would training be one-directional. Instead we would operate and coordinate with a cooperative teamwork mentality. The beauty and ease of my training philosophy is that it sets the goal of getting the dog to offer good behavior because it's rewarding for him to do so. The dog achieves success. So do you.

COOPERATION TRAINING

Cooperation training adjusts dogs' behaviors based on their instinctual rationale, which becomes linked to their way of learning. The compliant behavior developed by my techniques can be measured by a best-fit compatibility to an owner's lifestyle that doesn't strip a dog of his uniqueness. It was developed with the understanding that an owner cannot put twenty-three hours of a twenty-four-hour day into training a dog. Like you, I have an overscheduled and complex life. I can relate to the challenges of dog guardianship as both a trainer and a dog owner. The need for me to establish cooperative behavior from Sophie was imperative. She had to fit into my lifestyle, and I had to nurture her coping skills to reduce her anxiety.

It's always been clear to me that a militant training attitude puts too much pressure on the owner and the dog. I provide training techniques that can be integrated into normal, everyday activities. Essential to the process is establishing harmony in human-canine family dynamics. Canine drives, traits unique to individual dogs, owners' lifestyles and household setups all need to be balanced. My goal is to achieve an atmosphere of compatibility and support for both owners and dogs. My training techniques are designed to be rewarding for both ends of the leash.

Cooperation training takes a personalized approach. It considers all phases of a dog's life from puppyhood to the senior stage. It understands the challenges associated with training your dog when the relationship is strained and the doggy dynamics have gone awry. Whether dealing with housebreaking, leash aggression, separation anxiety, sibling rivalry or the arrival of a newborn infant, proper training is required. Other canine distress challenges—such as sensitivity to noise, crowds, places or objects—or setbacks attributed to a traumatic experience or other unknown causes, will need your commitment to resolve and modify the behavior.

Cooperation training seeks to resolve behavior issues by helping owners understand them from the dog's perspective, based on his instincts and canine-ality type. Reading a dog's behavior, not judging it, is how I coach an owner into understanding how dogs communicate with us. Too often dogs get mixed signals about their unwanted behavior. The dog that hasn't been taught boundaries does as he pleases because he believes you told him it was okay. No limits were set. He's on the couch, jumping on strangers or peeing in the house because he thinks it's acceptable behavior. "No" may have been said, but how was it said and, more important, how was it heard? You may have told him not to do something, but did you redirect his behavior to a desired one?

Owners often want help and they want their problems fixed right away. They want me to tell them what to do. When I explain it's what Fido wants as well, I usually get our first laugh. But it's true! He's saying, *"Tell me what to do!"* and he's working very hard to try to figure you out.

Perceptions about and reactions to circumstances differ among owners and their dogs. The human end of the leash may view something as uneventful, or even ordinary, while the dog's end may respond to the same stimuli with alarm. A delivery boy, or other service person, or a neighbor's child who grabs a tail, pulls an ear or pokes an eye may go unnoticed by an owner, but such a person can ignite a dog's sense of fear, or his protective impulse. Fido: *"He's trying to attack me. I'll growl, show him my teeth to make him stop."* When someone knocks on the door, he barks wildly to alert you. He's trying to warn or protect you, or maybe he's just excited about guests. How is he to know friend or foe?

Dogs' ears are perking up all over the world because they want to make you understand and experience life from their point of view. They're not bad dogs. More likely they're misunderstood, frustrated or bored.

Cooperation training targets puppies being housetrained and dogs that exhibit doorbell excitement or inappropriate guest greetings, such as jumping or nipping, that make anyone entering your home uncomfortable. Senior dogs, increasingly agitated and anxious because of medical conditions such as arthritis, decreased vision, loss of hearing or neuro-logical decline, can also benefit from training that recognizes and honors their stage in life.

CANINE-ALITIES

Canine-ality is a fun and interactive concept I developed to engage own-ers' curiosity about their dogs and their dogs' behaviors. It motivates owners to become creative, engaged and in sync with their dogs in order to achieve more rewarding relationships. Chapter 4 explains this con-

Kate Perry's Cooperation Training Canine-alities

- **Academic & Methodical Thinker**—These dogs always stop to think when a command is given.

- **Sensitive Artist**—Dogs, like people can be sensitive, reflective and reserved.

- **Workaholic**—This type isn't a wallflower. They're determined to get the job done. If you don't give them a job they'll assign one to themselves.

- **Party Animal**—"Born entertainers" describes these dogs' winsome canine-alities. Everything they do is with enthusiasm and a love of life.

cept geared toward advancing a training connection for both ends of the leash.

Discerning your dog's behavior is accomplished by developing an awareness of his canine-ality, not solely by generalizing about his breed type. This allows you to personalize your dog-training techniques and skills.

Having grown up in the Canary Islands, Greece and England rescuing all kinds of animals, including donkeys, rabbits, ducks, goats, cats, dogs and even a few fish, my instincts have become attuned to and in harmony with animals. Those valuable experiences left an indelible impression on me. My background has made me passionately interested in understanding people and animals. I always wanted to know who they were, what they needed and how I could help them. This fascination has come to shape and define me as a dog trainer skilled in knowing how to interpret canine behavior.

I see myself as a coach in the role of helping owners and dogs change the dynamics of their relationships. While training is about creating structure and routines, and maintaining consistency, there's no rule saying it can't be fun. LOOK-AT-ME is my bible command that also becomes a playful FOLLOW-THE-LEADER game. It's fundamentally important because it gets your dog to pay attention and tells him where to focus, while bringing a lively merriment to the training process.

By the time you finish this book, you will have a cooperative and personalized training routine that works for you and your dog. The techniques are intuitive and gentle. They are designed to fit easily into your life. Cooperation training is partnered training. It's suited for all needs because it's based on your dog's natural instincts and it adapts to your lifestyle.

Cooperation Training—success for both ends of the leash!

How to Understand Your Dog

The New York City Pet Expo ended on a warm spring day. Several of us in the pet business were on Eighteenth Street where cars, buses, bicycles, pedestrians, baby strollers, walkers and a hot dog vendor were all vying for street and sidewalk space. Suddenly, a black and tan dachshund jumped out of his carrier bag and bolted down the street, making a mad dash toward the oncoming traffic.

People started screaming as they scrambled to stop cars, trucks and motorcycles. The more chaotic the situation became, the more the dog darted between and under cars. He was feeding off fear and responding to the frenzied energy around him. Not good. The zigzagging, low-to-the-ground dachshund was all but invisible to motor vehicles. Shouts of "There's a dog loose!" got angry, expletive-yelling drivers to cooperate and understand what was at stake.

Instinctively switching mental gears, I became more dog-like in my thinking. "Stop chasing the dog, it's making him run. Remaining calm is the way to help him." Gaining everyone's cooperation, especially the dog's, was important. The dachshund did not think that people were coming to his rescue, but rather that they were threatening his existence. He was operating primarily off the canine drive known as "flight." Charging down the middle of the street was his defensive response to the perceived danger that stemmed from a high level of fear and anxiety. Understanding the canine drive of that dog in that moment was critical.

A drive is a dog's natural instinct that motivates his actions and reactions to people, places and things. The four prominent drives are: pack, prey, flight and fight. People chasing the dachshund were responding to their natural human instinct to help, but in the process they triggered the dog's complex flight drive. Also, if cornered, there was the potential of his fight drive taking over, though in that particular moment, it was all flight.

Using a clear, authoritative tone, I positioned myself in a leadership role. The communication channel for bystanders, dog and owner was no longer muddled with miscues and misunderstandings. I applied cooperation dog training techniques to the situation by encouraging the Manhattan crowd to work as a team toward a shared goal. Everyone was able to anticipate and coordinate actions because their roles were now defined.

An expansive human barrier was formed and the entire block was cordoned off. A calm energy replaced chaos and panic. Specific tasks were implemented, allowing the dachshund to become more in tune with his other drives. Waving his favorite toy out to him triggered his prey drive, which then assisted us in moving him in a desired direction. His owner standing in a key location elicited the pack drive—the desire to be near his family. With a strategy in place and a combined effort under way, a dog's life was saved.

Cooperation training takes into account that dogs don't reason the same way people do. They rely on their natural instincts (pack, prey, flight and fight) to learn how to thrive and survive. Illustrating canine drives in a story is how I teach owners to apply training techniques to meet the specific needs of their dogs. Understanding your dog starts with viewing his behavior and taking into account his prominent drives.

CANINE SPEAK

Dogs are predatory animals that use their body postures and facial expressions as a means of communicating (canine speak). The key to understanding how they think and react is through their body language and behaviors. Prior to domestication, dogs relied on their instincts and senses for survival. They had to expertly read the body language of others and be quick to respond. Today those skills are not used in the true predatory sense. Instead, dogs have mastered reading their owners' stances, tiniest mannerisms, behavioral habits, quirks, twitches and sounds as a way of interpreting what's expected of them.

Cooperation dog training teaches owners how to understand "canine speak." It breaks down the complex canine body language that encompasses a combination of subtle and obvious expressive gestures along with physical movements. Owners can improve communication, and therefore training, by paying attention to the actions and maneuverings of their dogs. Scientists, behaviorists and trainers categorize their behavior into displacement signals, cut-off signals and calming signals.

Behavioral Terms for Canine Communication

- **Displacement Behavior:** something a dog does when he feels uneasy or is trying to figure out what to do (fake scratch, sniff).
- **Calming Signal:** something a dog does to calm himself and the situation around him (yawning, lip smacking).

- **Cut-Off Signal:** something a dog does to end unwanted behavior (turning head to the side, walking away).

Note: Displacement, calming and cut-off signals are often overlapping behaviors. Deciphering the signals must take into consideration the context of a particular situation. A dog that yawns may be saying, *"I'm uncomfortable"* (displacement) or *"I want the other dogs around me to know I'm not a threat"* (calming signal). Cut-off signals are often easier for owners to interpret, as their intention is more direct in wanting to express a need to either escape or control a situation.

ACTIVE LISTENING

It's amazing that some dogs comply with their owners' wishes considering that the conversations most humans have with their dogs overlook how dogs actually speak to us. "Canine speak" is universal among dogs. All breeds negotiate greetings, desires and needs using a genetic-based, standardized language. To their credit, dogs are always trying to deduce, negotiate, respond to and even anticipate our requests. It's ironic that many owners feel their dogs ignore them when often it's the owner who is not listening. Active listening repairs breakdowns in communication. It develops a cooperative atmosphere that resolves unwanted behavior and advances training.

READING YOUR DOG

Most canine misbehavior can be attributed to a breakdown of communication. An owner can misinterpret a dog's attempt to inform or alert him about what's going on with the dog or his surroundings. For example, barking may seem offensive or annoying. On the other hand, the dog may be warning about an intruder entering your home. Even though you know there's no danger to your household, Scruffy has a different take: *"I let you know of a potential danger and get yelled at? Where's the 'atta boy' praise? I work 24/7 to maintain this household and get no respect."* Relationships are built on communication. A lack of understanding can lead to frustration and problems for both ends of the leash.

People are primarily verbal-centric in their communication, but dogs are not. Dogs speak to one another and to us through energized body and facial expressions (wagging tails, licking lips, tilting heads) as well as with pitches of vocalization (barks, growls, whimpers). Scent is another means of exchanging information, such as when dogs sniff one another. Dogs that smell urine and sniff butts glean information about gender, health, emotional states, arousal levels and territorial markings.

Since canine communication is derived from a dog's body, face, ears, tail, vocalizations and expressions, the best training advice for all owners is: watch to learn.

Generalized Body and Facial Expressions Translated into Canine Speak

Relaxed tail wag	*"I'm friendly"*
Stiff tail wag	*"I'm on guard"*
Tail tucked	*"I'm afraid"*
Eyes darting	*"I'm nervous"* or *"I'm anxious"*
Eyes staring	*"Don't mess with me"*
Ears pulled back	*"I'm scared"* or *"I'm concerned"*
Ears flickering forward	*"I'm curious"*
Mouth relaxed	*"I'm calm"*

Mouth tight, baring teeth. Low growl	*"Back off" or "I might bite"*
Body in freeze position	*"I'm conflicted and feeling fear" or "I might bite"*
Rolling on back with a relaxed, open mouth	*"Life is good"*

Displacement behavior and cut-off and calming signals are universal hardwired dog language. Dogs navigate their environments, resolve conflicts and use clever signaling to display stress, as well as goodwill, to other dogs and humans.

> Dog stares can be a complex behavior to read. If the dog's face and body are tense, this may be a warning or threat. Owners should look away from this type of canine direct stare. This presents a calming signal to a dog that you are not a threat to him. Err on the side of caution.

Displacement Behaviors and Cut-Off and Calming Signals

- Yawning
- Licking
- Shaking it off
- Scratching
- Fake sniffing
- Play bowing
- Eye darting

- Turning away
- Turning of head
- Walking slowly
- Freezing
- Smacking lips
- Wagging tail
- Sniffing
- Softening eyes
- Averting eyes
- Sitting
- Lying down
- Moving in an arc

PHYSICAL WORDS

Reading Canine Body Language ...
from head to tail!!!

Not every movement or expression constitutes a chat or a discussion. Some are reflexive. Sniffing can occur because your neighbor is grilling a steak. The point is to apply context and circumstances to your read on canine body language while understanding that dog language and dog thoughts are based on reactions to what they interpret as safe or dangerous situations. Even though domesticated, dogs still think in survival mode.

Understanding "canine speak" becomes critical when we want to curb, remove or interrupt a behavior we don't like. It can also be applied to help us shape or capture behavior we like and want to reinforce. To get cooperation from dogs, they need to be motivated to check in with their owners. The goal is to teach dogs to respond to owner commands anytime and anywhere, especially in new or stressful situations.

CANINE PERSPECTIVE

Cooperation dog training sees the world through a dog's eyes. Did you ever stop to think about how many doors you go through from the time you leave your home until you get outdoors, particularly if you live in an apartment or town house? Your front door, followed by the elevator door—in then out again—a foyer door, then finally the exit out the front door. All this before you reach the sidewalk. There's also the hallway and the passage through the lobby or common areas and, of course, the return trip. And how about the various floor surfaces your pooch may need to pad over, translate and cope with: wood, marble, carpet, linoleum, cement, pavement or other types of man-made or natural surfaces?

What about the elevator? How long do you and your pooch have to wait? Does your building allow dogs on the passenger car, or do you have to wait even longer for the freight elevator? Is it crowded? Does your pup react well to the confined space? Are there neighbors who don't like riding with pets? Are there children who are afraid of your dog, or lack gentle hands in approaching him? In a suburban setting, the weekend rituals of lawn mowing, leaf blowing and service deliveries may turn Fido into a raging, feisty pup or Scooter into a nervous wreck.

Hats, uniforms, canes, walkers and shoes that don't resemble shoes can all make your dog unsure, particularly if the contraptions squeak and scrape surfaces with irritating sounds in an inconsistent manner. Cooperation training can help turn canine fear into canine confidence through desensitization.

> The human end of the leash may view something as uneventful or even ordinary, while the dog's end may respond to the same stimulus with alarm.

LIFE'S REALITIES

Dogs need to be prepared for the realities of life and what they may present. The goal of training is to ensure that a dog's behavior is reliable under any circumstance and within all settings. "Canine stressors" is how I refer to "something coming around the corner." These stressors trigger the pack, prey, flight and fight drives of a dog. Cooperation training prepares owners to become aware of the stressors and use commands to redirect a dog's focus into desirable behavior.

Canine stressors can be managed using LOOK-AT-ME and TOUCH TARGET commands, which are explained in the next chapter. A dog lunging at a skateboarder or in reaction to a neighbor mowing his lawn can be reined in. Getting a dog's attention is crucial to training him.

CANINE STRESSORS SPECIFIC TO URBAN ENVIRONMENTS

OUTDOOR
- Garbage trucks
- Air brakes on buses or trucks
- Skateboards, rollerblades, wheelchairs and bicycles
- Doormen, policemen, UPS and other delivery people
- Other dogs in close proximity
- Walking on a leash
- Busy sidewalks
- Subway grates
- Noise, movement, pace, energy
- Traffic lights
- Jack hammering
- And more

INDOOR
- Small living spaces
- No backyard
- Elimination facilities limited to wee-wee pads
- House rules: "No barking," "off the couch," no furniture chewing & other restrictions
- Lobbies
- Elevators
- Neighbors
- Loneliness from long hours when owner is working
- Doorbells and knocks
- And more

CANINE STRESSORS SPECIFIC TO SURBURBAN & RURAL ENVIRONMENTS

OUTDOOR
- Wildlife (deer, fox, bear)
- Lawn mowers, leaf blowers
- Sprinklers
- Fencing and lawn ornaments
- Dog house
- Swimming pool
- Outdoor lights
- All terrain vehicles
- Snowmobiles
- Shotgun noise from hunters
- Chainsaw noise
- And more

INDOOR
- Doggy door & outdoor elimination areas
- Floor surfaces: marble, tile, carpeting, radiant-heated
- Limited interaction with other dogs and people
- Relaxed "No barking" rules
- Mudrooms
- Stairs
- Next-door neighbors
- Loneliness from long hours when owner is working
- Doorbells and knocks
- And more

EARNING A DOG'S TRUST

The dog every family desires got that way because a level of trust and reliable behavior was secured. Cooperation dog training establishes the groundwork for achieving owner and dog bilateral trust. Over time and with consistency, repetition and structure, trust is developed. It's earned and negotiated through simple acts that include the following:

- Setting a schedule (feeding, walking, exercise, playtime)
- Using specific word commands (LOOK-AT-ME, LEAVE IT, COME, GO PEE, etc.)

- Adhering to established house rules (Spot's bed location, the furniture policy, canine manners, etc.)
- Assuming a decisive and agreeable tone of voice and posture
- Using CORRECT (teaching a dog what not to do) and REDIRECT (teaching a dog what to do) commands

A dog wants to be inspired, encouraged and nurtured by a leader who clearly defines the dog's role in the family unit. If dogs are placed in circumstances where trust or consistency is lacking, they'll revert to their basic and primary instincts of pack, prey, flight and fight to problem-solve and survive. A challenge arises when the lack of trust induces behavior that manifests in the form of panic, anxiety or reactivity.

Mutual cooperation results from trust that's cultivated when owner and dog recognize, and are able to comply with, realistic expectations at both ends of the leash. Communication should be direct and timely. The goal of training is to create predictable and reliable behavior that's balanced and harmonious.

LEARN TO EARN

The "learn to earn" model makes a dog accountable for his actions and lets him know something is expected of his behavior. It also builds canine confidence and esteem while establishing an owner's leadership status. Mutual trust and respect is gained over time and expressed through consistent behavior. The dog taught to SIT prior to every meal earns his dinner. The SIT command becomes a rewarded behavior for a dog in the same way people go to work to earn a paycheck. He'll offer the behavior hoping for more money, i.e., treats or praise, and then be more responsive to SIT in other situations. SIT can advance to redirecting a dog from triggers such as another dog, a skateboarder or a siren. Since SIT is rewarding indoors, the chances are SIT outdoors will have the same impact.

The "learn to earn" model works because dogs have a primal need to eat. Hunger motivates compliance. Though with some dogs behavioral cooperation can be achieved with a toy or an activity, for the most part dogs, especially those on a strict work-to-eat program, will focus on their owner's commands and quickly figure out what they need to do to earn food. It's like people going to work to earn money so they can put food on the table. Once a challenging dog has become gainfully employed and been put under new management, he becomes less impulsive and more confident.

Using high-value treats or serving meals outdoors motivates a pooch to tune in to his owner, thereby advancing outdoor cooperation training.

TRAINING CONCEPTS AND TERMS

- **High-Value Reward:** Whatever is rewarding to your particular dog. Diced chicken cubes, freeze-dried liver, hot dog pieces or mozzarella cheese sticks are examples. Dick Van Patten's Natural Balance Rolls work well for many dogs, as do Cheerios for canines with weight issues or sensitive stomachs. Be sure to have treats readily available in small "easy access" pieces about the size of a dime. The key is to work with high-value treats that are small and easy for a dog to eat.

  A toy or play activity can be substituted if a dog is not treat-motivated. Prey-driven dogs may find a toy more motivating than food. In this case, choose a toy that will only be used in the training sessions. A canine favorite is a ball with a squeaky toy attached. That places a higher value on the toy and makes it more desirable.

Pack-driven dogs may find praise more rewarding than food or a treat.

- **"YES"**: The verbal cue used to mark and shape a desired behavior. "YES" informs the dog that he's done something right and the command has been successfully completed. It needs to be well timed to be effective. Think of it as the punctuation mark at the end of a sentence. Trainers sometimes use a clicker as an event marker. "YES" works just as well.

- **JOLLY EFFECT**: Dogs pick up on our energy, and they learn faster when not stressed. The JOLLY EFFECT is used when a known canine stressor—a street sweeper, vacuum or stranger— approaches and triggers fear, or a potentially aggressive response from your dog. For example, once the canine stressor comes into your radar (try to spot it before Fido does), change your vocal tone and energy to reflect joy and a relaxed disposition toward the stressor—whether it's an object, place or circumstance. When confronted with the canine stressor, let your dog witness your composure as something hip and fantastic. To build a positive association, give your dog a treat that's triggered by the event. For example: street sweeper = reward. Fido: *"When I see a street sweeper, something good happens for me. My owner thinks it's cool, which is kinda weird but whatever. Clearly there's nothing I need to worry about with street sweepers."*

- **JACKPOT REWARD**: Gambling is a good analogy for this method of training. A few small wins may motivate you, but hitting the jackpot keeps you playing and in the game for the rest of your life. The "JACKPOT" is the really big reward. It's when several high-value treats are given to your dog at a point in the training when a breakthrough moment of a shaped behavior occurs.

Jackpots should be linked with heartfelt verbal praise and happen at your discretion. The key is not to overdo them. Keep them in play as incentives. Sporadic and spread out jackpots keep the dog more interested in playing for Vegas odds.

- **Reality, Coordination, Timing and Proper Sequences:** It takes time to develop training techniques that feel natural to owners. Think of it as a process. Forming new ways of understanding canine behavior empowers owners to become the best advocates and trainers for their dogs.

  Patience is needed when developing coordination, decisive timing and the proper sequence of the command steps. The training process represents new behavior for both ends of the leash. Owners should be decisive when marking a dog's correct behavior after a command is given.

- **Consistency, Repetition and Structure:** Dogs acquire desired behaviors through consistency and repetition. Dogs, like children, need to be educated. Training teaches a dog what to do. Behavior problems can be avoided when owners provide dogs with structure and clear boundaries.

- **Generalization:** Dogs have the ability to apply learned knowledge to new places, situations and environments, but they don't generalize behavior very well. Just because a dog learns to sit in a kitchen doesn't mean he knows that he should sit in the living room or outdoors or in other locations.

  Desired behavior and taught commands need to be repeated, reapplied and relearned in many places and in lots of different situations in order to achieve reliable results. For example, a child who is taught table manners at home might revert to bypassing silverware in favor of using his hands to eat his food in a restaurant. A quick reminder gets him to realize (generalize) that wherever he eats, manners are required.

- **Threshold of Tolerance:** When a dog expresses his level of comfort toward various stimuli such as people, places and objects, including training sessions. Trainers often refer to this as a dog's workability range. A dog should never be pushed beyond his threshold of tolerance (comfort).

  Compromising a canine's threshold of tolerance can result in a loss of focus, decreased attention to commands, undesired reactiveness (e.g., yawning, licking, head turning) and even an emotional shutdown.

  Analogy: A toddler on the go all day without a nap and then taken to a gala will likely throw a tantrum during the event because he's exhausted beyond his threshold of tolerance.

Attention, Please

LOOK-AT-ME and TOUCH TARGET commands are direct and purposeful. They are the first two commands I teach to every dog I work with. I call them "Pay Attention" commands. They are the building blocks to more advanced commands. I equate them with teaching a child the ABC's before he can learn to read. Both are taught behaviors that quickly become conditioned and rewarding ones. These commands redirect a dog's state of mind. They can also be used to manage unwanted reactive behavior like barking, lunging and door charging. On the surface they may seem rudimentary, however, as your relationship with your dog evolves, they'll become the go-to commands used most often.

These commands could be lifesaving if a perilous situation were to arise. It could happen in a split second. Perhaps you are juggling some shopping bags, pushing a stroller or getting into a car when your dog unexpectedly pulls and his leash slips out of your hands. Gaining his attention with a LOOK-AT-ME or TOUCH TARGET at a time like that is crucial.

Both commands can also be used to teach your dog tricks like RING A BELL or HIGH FIVE. LOOK-AT-ME can also be used as a way to play FOLLOW-THE-LEADER. It supplies the answer to a dog's *"Tell me what to do"* request.

TOUCH TARGET, very much a GPS command, gives you the ability to navigate your dog around a chicken bone on the sidewalk or it can be converted to cueing him to a close heel position for a pleasurable stroll. We'll go into the command details soon, but first let's see how LOOK-AT-ME and TOUCH TARGET transformed one household.

NORMAN—"HE'S SOOOOOOOOO CUTE!"

Norman is an adorable, feisty and overly coddled corgi-terrier mix. He's a door charger. A knock on the door and he turns into a first responder deciding who enters, exits or is allowed to be near the entrance. He's convinced he's doing his job, but should a thirty-pound dog be the self-appointed arbitrator in our home? What are owners reinforcing by letting their dog dictate house rules? And what's next for Norman the Conqueror?

Norman: *"Door situation under control. Time to square up the rest of the territory and my objects: toys, food, couch*

LOOK-AT-ME and TOUCH TARGET redirects Norman's heightened behavior into managed and welcoming temperament.

and, well . . . yeah, why not take over the living room, kitchen and bedroom. I'll leave them with the bathroom. Also, as long as I'm on the 'mine rant'— the owners are mine. The other day in the elevator someone bumped up against my owners . . . My owners! I gave warning signs: shaking off, backing up and darting my eyes. Then I took action. It was a slight nip that settled the score. They got the message to back off. Next thing I know my owners are mad at me, saying, 'Bad dog!' Then seconds later they tell me, 'It's okay.' This is confusing so I respond to them in Robert De Niro fashion: 'You talkin' to me?' I mean really, I'm soooooooooooooo cute. That cracks them up and reminds them that I'm in charge of the household."

Without realizing it, the coddling actions of Norman's owners were reinforcing his tough-guy image. When working with Jenn and Brian, Norman's owners, I pointed out that they were missing a valuable training opportunity with him. "It's not okay" behavior began before Norman's elevator incident. The indicators were door charging and resource guarding. They first needed to redirect his behavior with LOOK-AT-ME and TOUCH TARGET training techniques to shift Norman's focus while changing his behavior. They had also fallen into the classic trap of boosting his bravado behavior with an "It's okay" sympathy pat given after altercations.

The chart below summarizes the disconnect between Norman's behavior and Jenn's and Brian's interpretations at both ends of the leash.

Behavior	Canine Thought	Owner Thought
Door charging	*"I'm on guard."*	"Yikes, that's annoying."
Sitting on couch staring at the door	*"Gotta protect . . . gotta protect . . . gotta protect . . . gotta protect!"*	"Oh, he wants to protect us. How sweet."

Couch nudger	*"My couch, my owner."*	"What a love bug."
Growling and nipping owner's hand during tug-of-war game	*"Don't mess with me."*	"He loves pretending to be a tough guy."
Hiding under the coffee table when guests arrive and occasionally popping his head out	*"Defense is ready and rarin' to go!"*	"That's so cute it's ridiculous."

Trainer's Thoughts on Norman the Conqueror

The dog that growls when you go near his food bowl, or freezes and sends a threatening look when anyone goes near his bed or bone is sending a warning to his owners. Door charging is a behavior that, left unchecked, easily escalates to varying degrees of aggression. The action signifies that he's controlling the household. In Norman's case, these behaviors were territorial and resource-guarding based.

If Norman's conduct were directed toward another dog, it would communicate, *"Stay away from my possessions and territory."* In the dog world, his species would pick up the canine cue and either respect it or challenge it. However, dogs are living on our home turf and need to abide by our rules and social constructs. That means we need to teach dogs acceptable responses to those situations. They need to be less affronting and more manageable. A dog's instinctive drive to survive needs to be corrected and redirected, and then replaced with rewarding cooperation-based behavior.

TALK TO ME

These commands help a dog figure out what an owner wants from him while channeling the dog's attention toward desired canine behavior. Both owner and dog work off each other's energy while learning to converse in an interspecies command-driven dialogue. Successful communication is bond-building and rewarding and accomplishes the goal of having a dog that's welcomed everywhere. Commands become learned language that enables owners and dogs to understand and cooperate with each other.

FEATURED TRAINING TECHNIQUES: LOOK-AT-ME AND TOUCH TARGET

Quick Description: LOOK-AT-ME

"PAY ATTENTION" is the message to your dog. This command develops a conditioned response to gain his focus. Checking in with his owner provides him with direction, reward and companionship. It establishes the FOLLOW-THE-LEADER behavior that's fun as well as motivational.

LOOK-AT-ME behavior is an immediate head turn from a dog so that his gaze connects with his owner. Whether a dog is standing, sitting or lying down, we want to train for a reliable and conditioned response to LOOK-AT-ME.

GOAL: LOOK-AT-ME establishes a bond and is used to manage and calm behavior.

LOOK-AT-ME Steps

1. Place a high-value treat in front of his nose and move it slowly to your eyes. As he follows the lure, use a light, happy tone and command, "LOOK-AT-ME." When he makes eye contact, mark the behavior with a clear and precise "YES," then treat and praise. Be quick to mark "YES."

2. Wait until he looks away before starting again. Repeat the exercise ten times before extending the length of time that the dog must look at you. When he's reliable at two seconds, graduate to three seconds.

LOOK-AT-ME, the Pay Attention command that gains a dog's focus and curbs unwanted behavior, puts Norman in his *"Tell me what to do"* mode.

3. When he responds quickly to the command, give a JACKPOT REWARD. Let him associate a fast response with a bigger reward.

4. Advance the command by adding in distractions, e.g., have a family member walk by or set your cell phone to ring and command, "LOOK-AT-ME." Turn this command into a reliable management tool for unexpected circumstances or when you need his attention right away (e.g., in an elevator or when a squirrel darts by).

5. Repeat this exercise in at least five to ten different locations inside and outside your home and neighborhood.

DELAYED REWARD

Delaying the reward is also a way to start weaning a dog off treats. Early in the training process, treats serve as motivation to gain a dog's focus. Treats are used as lures (incentives) to shape behavior by guiding a dog into a command. When a reliable response to a command happens, the next step is to delay the reward and establish his impulse control and alertness.

The DELAYED REWARD training game is based on consistency, patience and trust between an owner and his dog. The message to Fido is: "The reward is coming, be patient and stay focused. Patience is the behavior I want." Patience then transforms into a rewarding behavior.

> DELAYED REWARD is a technique that advances training. It prevents a dog from exhibiting demanding behavior and is part of teaching him good manners.

Advancing LOOK-AT-ME Using DELAYED REWARD Step

1. Pretend to have in your hand the treat that lures your dog's attention. In the other hand have a JACKPOT REWARD.
2. Command LOOK-AT-ME and when he responds, mark it with "YES." This time show him the empty hand for two or three seconds (delayed reward), then take the other hand with the jackpot and give it to him.

Quick Description: TOUCH TARGET

"TELL ME WHAT TO DO!" command. It establishes clear and concise direction, telling him where to target his attention.

TOUCH TARGET is the decisive command for reining in a dog's focus and behavior.

It's a command with practical and fun applications that establishes good canine manners and easily adapts to tricks like ringing a bell to tell an owner he needs to go the bathroom.

TOUCH TARGET is the building block command for advanced commands such as DROP IT and LEAVE IT.

TOUCH TARGET Steps

1. Place a treat in your hand and use your thumb to secure it like a dispenser. Turn your hand over, revealing the palm side face forward to create a touch target area for your dog's nose.

2. With the smell of the treat he'll be lured to sniff your hand. If needed, wave the hand with the treat near the dog's nose. Once his attention is moving toward the hand, command, "TOUCH." When his nose makes contact with the hand, say, "YES," and treat.

   Note: "TOUCH" is the luring action and "YES" (event marker) is the completion of the desired behavior.

TOUCH TARGET is a building block command that reestablishes trust at both ends of the leash. Jenn works the command with Norman.

3. Repeat this exercise ten times in at least three different locations in your home.

4. Now increase the distance between you and your dog and repeat the exercise ten times. Again, do so in at least three different locations in your home.

TRAINING TECHNIQUES SPECIFIC TO NORMAN

LOOK-AT-ME relieves Norman of his *"I'm in charge"* attitude. His owners take the lead and build on this command to gain their dog's attention and focus in all situations and circumstances. TOUCH TARGET is not the complete answer to resource guarding. That's a much larger topic. However, TOUCH TARGET does help to redirect Norman's behavior.

Norman and his owners now work with a dynamic, win-win approach. They capitalized on the strength of Norman's pack drive by using the Pay Attention commands. And the underlying component of mutual cooperation, best serving both ends of the leash, is rewarded and reinforced with LOOK-AT-ME and TOUCH TARGET. Norman: *"My 'You talkin' to me?' had to do with canine insecurity. I felt I needed to be in charge but that's not the case. It's more relaxing to turn to my owners to gauge what my response should be in all situations."*

LOOK-AT-ME and TOUCH TARGET build a bond of trust. Norman receives a higher-value treat and praise for redirecting his responses to his owners' commands. The TOUCH TARGET incentive gets Norman to rethink his actions because he is compensated for acceptable behavior. He will learn not to guard his toys if he's taught that they can be exchanged for treats.

Three Phases of Learning

1. **Learning:** Owner and dog master an understanding of commands. An owner needs to be patient and focused on rewarding the desired behavior, not mistakenly reinforcing unwanted behavior. A dog needs a calm environment to work in without distractions.

2. **Distraction:** Noise, movement and obstacles are added to the process to foolproof the behavior. During this phase, owners fine-tune their body language and vocal tone to provide clear and decisive communication to their pets. The goal is for commands to become reliable and generalized.

3. **Maintenance:** Training is for a dog's entire life span. What's great about cooperation dog training is that the commands we learn can evolve into games and lifestyle training techniques.

Don't Leave Home Without Them

Training starts by teaching a dog to check in with his owner. LOOK-AT-ME and TOUCH TARGET are two user-friendly commands that instantly change and manage your relationship with your dog. These foundation commands start the training engine and could adopt (and modify) the American Express tagline to: "Don't leave home without them." By following my techniques, everyone in your dog's inner circle, including children, housekeepers and guests, can implement the Pay Attention commands without feeling overwhelmed. LOOK-AT-ME and TOUCH TARGET teach a dog to trust his owners and understand that they are always in charge.

What's Driving the Relationship?

Meet Tucker, a three-year-old rescue. The talk bubble over this Jack Russell terrier wasn't "Chicken, please!" Instead it read like the verdict of a man wrongly convicted of a crime: "I don't want to talk about it. I SAID . . . I DON'T WANT TO TALK ABOUT IT." Sometimes the caption above his head said nothing, nothing at all. That was worse. There was no warning to those around him that he'd strike out at them.

Tucker came into Caryl and Gary's life exhausted from what life had been prior to his new home. For the first two weeks he mostly slept. When Tucker finally began to adjust to his surroundings, his baggage from being abused came out. The shut-down dog was a terror. He was an aggressor and a biter, revealing a layer of his personality that was alarming. The charming and more likable aspects of his disposition were hidden behind his defensiveness.

Tucker is an extreme case. Because he was a rescue, there's no history to help us understand how his reactive behavior developed. Something bad must have happened to him in a kitchen. His reactions and haunting flashbacks seemed to manifest in nanoseconds, especially in that room. However, Tucker was not without a totally affectionate side. He loved rolling on his back and letting his owners indulge in a love fest with him. Yet his Jekyll and Hyde temperament placed Caryl and Gary at risk of being bitten.

One of the goals of cooperation training is to ensure a dog's behavior is reliable under any circumstances and within all settings. It's

Tucker's owners never anticipated that rescuing him would be a complicated situation.

also about providing a dog with coping skills to reduce his stress. Most people would have given up on this dog after two days, but Tucker's owners are exceptional. It took about six months of training to bring about a transformation that changed the lives at both ends of the leash. Everyone will find their own path in training that works for them, and for these owners, it all began with a survey.

PERSONALIZED TRAINING PROGRAM

Every dog is different, but by assessing a dog's dominant drives and canine-alities, we can create a personalized training program to promote good behavior and overcome obstacles. This can be achieved with the Canine Drive Survey, which is made up of forty questions relating to the four drives: pack, prey, flight and fight. Understanding a dog's instincts will help you to comprehend your pet's reactions and behaviors.

The survey engages owners in the training process. Their answers to the survey place canine behaviors into drive categories, providing a frame of reference for owners to view the world from their dogs' perspective.

While all dogs exhibit these four drives at one time or another, most dogs have an inclination toward one, or maybe two, of them. Besides owners, it is helpful if those in your pet's inner circle also take the survey so you gather as much information as possible. The answers to the survey questions reveal the prominent drives that trigger your dog's behavior.

Results are shared and compared to provide an objective evaluation of the dog's primary drives and his behaviors associated with them. The feedback from the surveys is then applied to develop targeted training techniques for your dog. It connects owners to training techniques and methods best suited to their dogs' temperament. Survey scores often vary within a dog's inner circle. It simply means that he may alter his behavior based on how he's being handled at the other end of the leash, or he may respond differently to his "pack" members.

THE ANSWERS ARE
IN THE QUESTIONS

The following survey is my version of a commonly used questionnaire that many trainers use to help owners determine their dogs' prominent drives. Unique to my take on the survey is that I adapted and modified it to work in tandem with canine-ality types discussed in the next chapter. The aim of the survey is for owners to recognize that dogs respond differently and uniquely to the stresses of life. A dog's threshold of tolerance for stress, his environment and other factors is set off and influenced by his dominant canine drive.

How to Take the Canine Drive Survey

Read through each of the following drive categories and give each behavior a score. Score behaviors as follows: 1-3 = rarely; 4-6 = occasionally; and 7-10 = frequently. Then tally the score for each drive.

The tallies are a guide to how a dog responds to and operates in the world around him. Specific training techniques can then be matched to enhance or reduce drives. Scores above 75 and below 25 in a particular drive provide owners with the awareness of their dogs' training needs.

Repeating the survey frequently charts the training achievements and helps to reveal any adjustments or modifications that may need to be made to the training techniques. I advise owners to repeat it monthly.

Pack

The motivating trait prompting dogs to follow owners. A dog with a strong pack drive is nicknamed "Velcro dog" because its preference is always to be in the company of its owners. This dog will follow you everywhere, including the bathroom.

Does your dog:

1. Follow you everywhere? ____
2. Like people in general (doormen, strangers, delivery people, passersby, etc.)? ____
3. Like or love being handled and stroked? ____
4. Bring you toys to solicit play? ____
5. Like gazing into your eyes for long periods of time? ____
6. Enjoy the company and interaction of other dogs on- and off-leash? ____

7. Greet you or others exuberantly by jumping on you or them? ____

8. Enjoy and welcome being groomed? ____

9. Seek opportunities to play with other dogs on- or off-leash? ____

10. Vocalize by barking or whining when left alone? ____

Pack Drive Total: ____

Prey

A dog's survival and arousal instinct to scavenge (hunt) for food and chase after objects, people and other animals. Note: Wheelphobia, a dog's reaction to all things wheels, brings out a dog's predatory heightened re-activity to movement. It's a prey and territorial response.

Does your dog:

1. Stalk animals like squirrels, pigeons, cats, dogs, rodents, deer or other wild critters? ____

2. Carry items or toys around in your apartment or backyard? ____

3. Shake toys energetically in his mouth? ____

4. Steal food or items from countertops or tables, or forage through garbage? ____

5. Consume food rapidly? ____

6. Become excited by the movement of bikes, skateboards, children running, etc.? ____

7. Bury his bones or hide his toys? ____

8. Tirelessly retrieve balls and Frisbees? ____

9. Turn into an obsessive sniffer on walks outside? ____

10. Pounce on or attack his toys? ____

Prey Drive Total: ____

Flight

A new or unfamiliar situation can cause this dog to want to run away, hide or cower. Street sweepers, thunderstorms and fireworks often prompt fearful reactions.

Does your dog:

1. Immediately respond (react) to new situations and scenarios by running away or hiding from them? ____
2. Urinate during a meet-and-greet situation? ____
3. Cower, shake or tremble when someone bends over him? ____
4. Air-bite or snap when stressed, cornered or pushed beyond his threshold of tolerance? ____
5. React fearfully to startling noises such as thunder, construction sounds and raised voices? ____
6. Shake or whine when stressed in your home or outside? ____
7. Submissively turn his back when corrected? ____
8. Have a tendency to walk timidly behind you on walks? ____
9. Hesitate when you call him to come to you, or leave some distance between the two of you when he does come? ____
10. Move around and pant a great deal while being groomed? ____

Flight Drive Total: ____

Fight

When a dog perceives a threat and reacts by lunging or barking. Survival tends to be the underlying catalyst for this drive.

Does your dog:

1. Charge at the door when someone knocks? ___
2. Guard and become possessive of toys, food or other things (purse, bed, couch, etc.) inside or outside? ___
3. Provoke fights or try to dominate other dogs? ___
4. Become overly protective of you or other family members? ___
5. Become territorial about his home, bed, doorway, couch, front stoop or dog carrier? ___
6. Not enjoy being handled, petted or groomed? ___
7. Keep you on high alert during walks knowing that he'll likely lunge unprovoked at other dogs? ___
8. Play tug-of-war and wrestle with a must-win attitude? ___
9. Become reactive toward unfamiliar objects or sounds like skateboards, street sweepers, lawn mowers, vacuum cleaners, etc.? ___
10. Easily growl in low bass-like tones under the least amount of stress? ___

Fight Drive Total: ___

Tucker's Canine Drive Survey Scores			
PACK: 30	PREY: 95	FLIGHT: 10	FIGHT: 95

CANINE DRIVES

Canine behavior reflects inborn temperament that is derived from the four primal drives: pack, prey, flight and fight. The mesmerizing, hilarious and zany shenanigans of a litter of eight-week-old puppies in a whelping pen or pet store captures our hearts, hitting the adorable button over and over again. With their chubby bellies, puppies race, tumble and spin as they turn shredded newspaper into celebratory canine confetti.

They also act and behave in ways that demonstrate the four principal canine drives: One chases his siblings (prey); another roams, but always with other puppies (pack); a third tough-guy loves to growl and is full of antics (fight); and the fourth, the one being ambushed by tough-guy, takes off running (flight). Though a certain pup may have a stronger tendency to work off a pack, prey, flight or fight drive, each dog comes fully loaded with all four. They're all there, like a person's mood swings. Understanding a dog's inclination toward one drive over another helps raise an owner's awareness of his pet's reactions (behaviors) toward people, places and things.

At eight to sixteen weeks of age and away from littermates, and now in your own home, the puppyhood capers of tug-of-war games (prey), shadowing you around the house (pack), nipping at your ankles (fight) or getting timid around new people or other puppies (flight) seem typical and acceptable. But they're also a precursor of what's to come if we don't understand the implications of our dog's dominant drive and address it. A strong pack drive can be fabulous unless it leads to separation anxiety, and the consequences of an extreme fight drive not kept in check can be costly and heartbreaking. Here's where the survey comes in.

START WITH A BLANK SLATE

Owners need to compile a pet profile that's authentic and useful, not biased. Start with a blank slate by removing labels such as: "Brando is timid." "Rufus is a bully." "Penny is obstinate." Or "All pit bulls are aggressive and all Labradors are friendly."

Dogs don't hold grudges or become resentful. They don't seek to punish owners. Feeling guilty for going out to dinner with friends is in your head, not his. Kala, a Rhodesian ridgeback, didn't destroy the couch cushion because she wanted to teach you a lesson. Research studies have shown dogs are not wired to think that way.

What's driving the behavior is a dog's unique temperament as it relates to the world around him. It's important to resist humanizing your dog's behavior. Many factors, including genetics, the environment and an owner's lifestyle, influence a dog's behavior.

REALIZATIONS, NOT HUMANIZATIONS

Taking the quiz removes the tendency to humanize dog behavior and replaces it with a user-friendly approach that embraces the science of animal learning theory. Owners learn to recognize and translate subtleties of canine communication known as **displacement behavior** and **calming signals**, which include things like licking lips and yawning. The survey organizes owners' observations into the categories of pack, prey, flight and fight. This becomes the starting point in the training process where an owner begins to understand how to read dog language.

"Learning to read our dog's body language was key for us. We didn't understand Tucker's signals. Both of us have been around dogs our entire lives, but that didn't prepare us for Tucker. The survey put his behaviors into a context we could relate to. His behavioral warnings, like turning his head with a growl or flinching at a hand over his head, were his way of communicating," said Caryl and Gary.

Before taking the survey, Tucker's owners knew that reaching over his head or grabbing his collar, especially in the kitchen, set him off. He'd bite. The specific cause that triggers his fight drive is largely unknown. Tucker doesn't like eye contact (pack drive), whereas he tirelessly enjoys retrieving balls and other toys (prey drive), and he becomes territorial, provokes fights with other dogs and keeps his owners on high alert during walks (fight drive).

Other realizations that came to light from the survey were that Tucker would freeze in place before incidents, and that the kitchen area and certain times of day set him off. Also the owners were at risk whenever they had to put anything over his head, such as a harness, a sweater or a towel to dry him off after a bath or rainstorm. Finally, they were also on high alert on the streets, in their lobby, on the beach and elsewhere because he was always ready to confront other dogs.

MANAGE THE SITUATION

After taking the survey, Caryl and Gary shared a similar read on Tucker. Both surveys indicated that fight and prey were his dominant drives. The commands to focus on with Tucker would be those that enhanced his pack drive and curbed his fight and prey drive as much as possible, especially during daily walks. We also wanted the commands to be integrated and reliable to help build trust and strengthen the bond at both ends of the leash. A desensitization and counterconditioning program was also necessary. More about that in chapter 9.

Tucker's freezing in position was comparable to another dog's growling. Caryl and Gary first needed to manage the situation by respecting the silent warning. In that moment, not handling Tucker was important. We then worked to counter that behavior by increasing his pack drive with modified versions of the commands LOOK-AT-ME and TOUCH TARGET. In order to reduce Tucker's reaction to having people lean over him or place anything above his head, Caryl and Gary tweaked their stance when addressing Tucker. Providing these commands in a non-threatening posture helped to build a bond of trust. He'd comply because this Jack Russell loved being given a task, showing off his "workaholic" canine-ality.

Cooperation training techniques are flexible and adapt to reflect owners' unique household and lifestyle needs.

SHERLOCK CANINE HOLMES

Early in the training process, emotions can run high. Sorting them out is about engaging an owner while providing insight, not just parceling out training tips and techniques. Becoming the Sherlock Canine Holmes for your dog is another way, like the survey, that makes owners curious about their dog in a new way. Detailed questions are asked to get to the root cause of the problem with logic, not emotion. What were the owners doing at the time of Tucker's outburst? Did Tucker's body language in those moments provide clues? How did the owners and dog react afterward?

Dogs also learn to become detectives in the training process. They are trying to figure us out. After I coached Caryl and Gary to include an aloof training game protocol to lower Tucker's fight drive and increase his pack drive, Tucker started asking his own Holmes-like questions, such as: *"How do I get food?"* and *"What do I have to do to get your attention?"* Dogs become very responsive when they realize they need you to survive. My Sherlock Canine Holmes technique keeps training interesting for both ends of the leash.

ALOOF GAME
TAILORED TO TUCKER

Caryl had sustained a bite from Tucker that left him traumatized. To reboot the dynamics, and lower Tucker's fight drive, I had Caryl become the "hunter" providing food for Tucker's survival. It's a primal strategy consistent with the way a dog thinks while building a dependency and connection with his owner. The steps were to hand-feed Tucker and then become aloof and reserved around him. The standoffish energy changed the *"Who's in charge?"* bravado that Tucker had employed. His fight drive was lowered around Caryl, and what Tucker gained was a cooperative spirit that positioned his owner as a friend, not a foe. Whenever Tucker showed his Hyde temperament, Caryl ignored him. Tucker then had to rethink how to get his and Gary's attention.

TRAINING TECHNIQUES SPECIFIC TO TUCKER

Six months into training, there was a significant increase in Tucker's pack drive. The survey boosted Caryl and Gary's confidence. They began to see themselves as the trainers for their dog. Leadership and cooperative behavior stemmed from a strong foundation of trust. Tucker found it more rewarding to rely on his pack drive, rather than on his fight drive. The survey helped these owners figure out what Tucker needed and how to give it to him. Retaking the Canine Drive Survey as often as needed is the best way to keep on top of training.

Outdoors, the LOOK-AT-ME command was, for a time, difficult and agitating for Tucker. Triggers, such as dogs, noises, people, wheels or anything that made him uneasy, challenged his attention. TOUCH TARGET tackled Tucker's dislike of eye contact and still accomplished gaining his focus while rechanneling his behavior. Added to the equation was adjusting the tall owners' stances to work around Tucker's reaction to having people lean over him or place anything above his head. Using a sideways version of TOUCH TARGET further reduced the risk of triggering Tucker. Both adjustments—changing of the owners' physical stance and applying a sideways TOUCH TARGET—were key in setting up both ends of the leash for success. TOUCH TARGET was a doable command that encouraged Tucker to make contact with his owners using his nose, not his mouth. This also was an effective way to begin subtle work with Tucker on bite inhibition. Implementing win-win dynamics is central to cooperation training.

Tucker's sideways TOUCH TARGETs are brilliant. He's a doer. His attitude is: *"Got that—fine, fine, now please tell me what to do next."* These clever owners even embraced advanced commands in order to adapt to the Tucker-isms of not wanting to be touched. After a rainstorm or a walk in the snow, for example, they taught him to spin around on a preheated plush towel to accomplish hands-free paw cleaning. This trick also complements his *gotta-do* Jack Russell work ethic.

Why was Tucker compliant? Because for a food-motivated Jack Russell that loved being given a task, there was a reward for his good behavior. With patience and by using commands such as TOUCH TARGET, Tucker's human-canine bond was rebooted. The technique presented an innovative way for the two ends of the leash to relate to each other. When Tucker touched his nose to his owners' hands, he felt no threat. This consistent, repetitive action became a reinforcement and motivational reward that built up his trust. At the same time, the owners gained confidence in a training intervention designed to bring out the more cooperative and appealing sides of Tucker's personality.

> True leadership is about inspiring and encouraging confidence in ourselves and in our dogs. A confident dog is better behaved and more relaxed. Dogs need to know their owners are in control of the world around them.

END ON A GOOD NOTE

Once a social misfit without friends, Tucker has made a positive transition. "Dutchy, a docile female chocolate Lab, is our neighbor's dog," said Caryl. "We've known the neighbor for a long time, but for her dog's safety, we kept both dogs apart. One day I was in my driveway with Tucker when Dutchy ran across the street. It's very rural here and it happened so fast. Tucker looked at her, nipped her and barked. Dutchy returned with a play bow and turned her side to Tucker. It was so simply done, and they've been inseparable ever since. Dutchy gave our dog an *'It's all okay'* sign, in a language both dogs understood. That's not going to happen with every dog, but it happened with Rocko, a King Charles [male, Manhattan native], a Boston terrier he met on the street and a Cavalier that he met on the beach. More recently he got a new pal named Buddy."

Gary shared, "Tucker had special needs and we needed a special education to help us connect to him. We changed our mind-set and realized that we couldn't compare him to our past dogs. We had to respect him as a dog and understand what being a dog really meant."

Tucker's story embraces the heart of cooperation dog training: the bond between owner and dog, and the goal of becoming the best trainer for your dog. Adhering to the process (owner compliance) and expending the necessary effort is critical. The series of commands, like LOOK-AT-ME and TOUCH TARGET, establish a mutual language for owner and dog. They tell a dog what to do and how best to interpret what's being asked of him. Consistency and repetition in handling further fosters the bond between an owner and his dog. The owner's insight into how best to guide a dog into cooperating with commands is gained through the Canine Drive Survey. Understanding what's driving your dog's behavior is what develops targeted and personalized training techniques to meet the specific needs of your dog.

Training for Connection

When you're looking for a dog, you may not be thinking about a relationship. Nevertheless getting a dog is about finding and connecting with a new mate. If you get lucky, you and your dog will be a perfect match. If not, don't worry. Personality/canine-ality mismatches are quite common. They can work because there are training techniques to help you navigate the rough patches. Think of it as couples counseling for the two- and four-legged crowd. The process of working things out begins by discovering who your dog is and who you are to your dog.

Personality clashes happen at work, in the home and in social situations. These encounters can engender anxiety, insecurity, misunderstandings and frustration. With a dog, it becomes problematic when the perceived agreeable pocket pooch, intended to be a take-everywhere pal, turns out to be a bossy and reclusive drill sergeant. Or, conversely, when an eighty-seven-pound rottweiler establishes the goal of being a permanent lap dog.

In this chapter, we continue to focus on basic obedience commands while enhancing the connection between you and your dog.

TOMATO TOMÄTO COUPLES

Ollie, a rescued Australian cattle dog mix, and his owners, Desmond and Andrew, are a classic mismatch. Theme music from the TV show *The Odd Couple* could appropriately play softly in the background for this matchup. The owners' personalities and lifestyle were polar opposites to Ollie and his needs. Desmond, an editor, likes to read and considers himself a curmudgeon. Sitting and writing summarize his exercise routine. His partner, Andrew, works in finance. Home is his place to unwind and get away from his fast-paced job. Ollie is a tornado that tears through your living room.

Ollie and Desmond share a cultural exchange called
"Bow, Wag and Shake Paw."

"I didn't think we were ready to get another dog," said Desmond. "Coco, a sixteen-year-old basset-corgi mix, had died one day shy of a year ago on the very day that Andrew donated her things to Mighty Mutt Rescue. On the way home, he passed a parked North Shore Animal League van on the corner of our street. Returning home, he couldn't wait to tell me, 'I saw this puppy.' I shook my head no and meant it. An hour later we proceeded to the outdoor shelter van to take a look, but he didn't tell me which dog. Then 'No' changed to 'That's the one.' I remember picking him up and putting him on my shoulder. Whatever he needed—anything—he was going to get."

Without realizing it, these methodical-thinking owners, reserved and soft-spoken, had committed to raising a whirlwind, workaholic and party animal pooch.

CANINE-ALITIES

My methodology gets to the heart and soul of a dog, his canine-ality. As mentioned in the introduction, canine-alities are a combination of genetic influences, a dog's capacity to learn and his particular circumstances (his household, owner's lifestyle, etc.). They help owners to understand and modify canine behavior. In this chapter, I help you identify canine-alities as a means of guiding you to become the best trainer for your dog. The four primary canine-ality types demonstrate the motivational factors that prompt the actions of individual dogs. Read the following descriptions of canine-alities and consider how you might describe your own canine friend.

What's Your Dog's Canine-ality?

- **Academic and Methodical Thinker**—These dogs stop to think when a command is given. Charlie, a chocolate Labrador, lives in a densely populated section of Soho. He was taught to ring a bell when he needed to go outside to pee or poop, and he learned to go to his bed on cue. When a command was given, you could almost hear his brain working overtime to figure out what was being asked of him. His expressions would remind you of a person figuring out a crossword puzzle or thinking through a math problem.

- **Sensitive Artist**—Dogs can be sensitive, reflective and reserved. Beignet is a golden retriever living in the East Village in Manhattan. The loud sounds and rough play of puppy class were too much for him. He'd roll on his back to say, *"No threat—I'm not a threat."* Beignet is like the artist child who feels completely out of place with the jocks at school.

- **Workaholic**—This type isn't passive. They're determined to get the job done. If you don't give them a job, they'll assign one to themselves. Like Trixie, a border collie, did. When her owner arrived home, Trixie demonstrated her interior decorating skills by having chewed off the last leg of the chaise lounge. Ta-da—she was done and very pleased with the remodeling job. These are go-getters with energy that doesn't quit. A game of fetch could start in the morning and go until midnight.

- **Party Animal**—"Born entertainers" describes these dogs' winsome canine-ality. Everything they do is with enthusiasm and a love of life. They're ready to partake in whatever you have planned for them because, after all, it's one big party. Think lovable class clowns with a touch of wisecracking Looney Tunes characters packed into fur suits that entertain you daily with their shenanigans. When the doorbell rings they bark, twirl in circles and jump at the prospect of the more the merrier. Their motto: Let's get this party started!

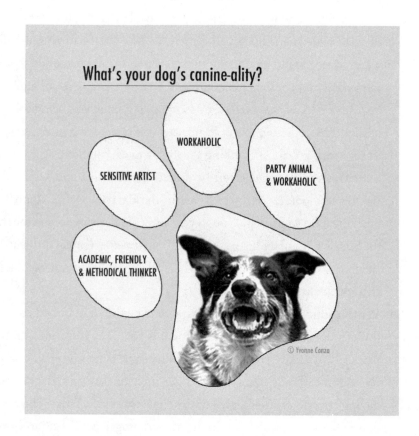

What's your dog's canine-ality?

WORKAHOLIC

SENSITIVE ARTIST

PARTY ANIMAL & WORKAHOLIC

ACADEMIC, FRIENDLY & METHODICAL THINKER

© Yvonne Conza

WORKAHOLIC–PARTY ANIMAL

Workaholic–Party Animal. That was my first impression of Ollie. He's straight from a Wild West Show. This dog could make Richard Branson look lazy and unoriginal. He had a workhorse "What's next?" pulsating energy that correlated to his canine-ality.

As with the four canine drives, dogs can exhibit combinations of canine-alities. Dogs are often multifaceted and able to express all four sides of canine-alities: methodical thinker, sensitive artist, workaholic and party animal. Owners can even be innovative and discover unique canine-alities that match their dog. For example, he's a quirky player or a conscientious organizer. It all depends on the situation, environment and relationship. Most dogs are inclined toward one or maybe two of them.

Desmond and Andrew had wanted a dog to become a part of their family. They weren't looking for one to change their lives. This 180-degree-turnaround owner-dog story involves two methodical thinkers, one workaholic–party animal, running shoes, a powerful bond and a co-operative, reciprocal leash connection.

"After we brought Ollie home, we realized that he had a fascination with his new puppy teeth," said Desmond. "He liked trying them out on everything! Balls and toys belonging to other dogs in the park and elsewhere were a problem. He wanted them. Also, herding Andrew and chasing the vacuum were becoming favorite Ollie activities. We needed a trainer right away." The quick read on Ollie: "Needs job and loves to party."

Dogs have many layers to their canine-alities. For Desmond and Andrew, it was all about getting to know their dog as an individual—all his quirks, habits, mannerisms and even flairs of eccentricity. A canine-ality type, like the survey, is a training tool. When owners are introduced to canine-ality types, they advance to personalizing the process and having fun with the dog training techniques.

HUMAN TYPES

Consider your own canine-ality, or rather your personality. This tends to be a lightbulb moment for the owners I work with. Think about your lifestyle and the impact dog ownership is having on it. The connection between canine drives, canine-alities, lifestyles and more begins to make sense when you examine all aspects of the situation and explore the differences from a fresh perspective.

It wasn't easy for methodical owners Desmond and Andrew to step out of their comfort zone. Being authoritative and setting down rules was challenging for them. They had to become decisive leaders for Ollie. They also had to negotiate his work ethic while balancing his party-animal needs as they related to training techniques.

"I remember taking Ollie to the dog run for the first time and thinking, 'I have to go in there with all those people?' Dog runs can be intimidating places with tight-knit groups and cliques," said Desmond. Ollie, known as the unofficial "mayor" of his neighborhood, pushed Desmond to expand his social skills. "The socializing thing was probably the most difficult for me because I like my privacy. Coco, our previous dog, never stopped and greeted other dogs or people, but Ollie loves every dog and everyone. He's even got folks on the block that he sees every day—he *must* see them."

TRAINING TECHNIQUES SPECIFIC TO OLLIE

"It's working! Ollie cooperates with us, not just when we train him, but in general," remarked Desmond and Andrew after Ollie completed puppy, basic and intermediate classes with me. In addition, they had arranged private sessions for him to tackle specific issues. This savvy household had become aware that dog behavior results from a combination of factors. They stayed on top of his training.

Ollie needed to know what was expected of him and that meant Desmond and Andrew being specific with their commands. These methodical thinkers turned into inspiring leaders who were no longer reserved in their training approach. They revamped their techniques. Achieving the desired training results came from them being firm, decisive and encouraging.

"The most important thing we have learned is consistency. Be consistent. DOWN is DOWN and don't say DOWN three times. Say it once. Telling a dog, 'SIT, SIT, SIT,' teaches the dog that the SIT command must be repeated three times before he should sit. Another confusing command is SIT DOWN. Which action are you asking from your dog? 'SIT'? or 'DOWN'? Being consistent and decisive with your commands matters."

Leadership Tips for Becoming the Best Trainer for Your Dog

1. Believe and have confidence in yourself as a trainer for your dog.
2. Have a vision and establish doable goals.
3. Maintain a tone of voice that's firm, precise and nonthreatening.
4. You and members of your dog's team need to be decisive with commands. Training is all about repetition and consistency.
5. Leading means making adjustments as needed, or based on circumstances requiring a new direction or a fresh approach.
6. Remember: Leaders inspire and encourage followers.
7. Listen to your instincts and trust your gut.

FEATURED TRAINING TECHNIQUE: SIT

Quick Description: SIT

SIT is a common courtesy command similar to shaking hands when people first meet. It's the *"I'm listening"* and *"Please"* position for what's next, such as a meal, a walk or a trip to the dog run.

SIT is a good command to use at red lights or around small children who could easily be knocked down by an excitable dog.

SIT Steps

1. Place a yummy treat between your thumb and index finger, then position it in front of your dog's nose. Slowly move the treat first toward his eyes, then his forehead, between his ears and finally toward the back of his neck. The dog will instinctively follow the motion of the food.

2. As his head goes back and his behind hits the floor, say, "YES," and give him the treat.

3. If you have an excited, high-energy pooch, the food lure needs to be worked slowly with repetitions.

4. If the dog tries to jump up to the hand with food, stay still and give him five seconds to lose interest in jumping and return to sitting. If that doesn't happen, go back to step 1. Be patient. Take a break before starting over and then resume the SIT command for ten repetitions.

5. Once the dog has become a sitting machine, start adding the language SIT as you lure him into position. Take the treat out of your

hand and use the same lure motion over his head while rising to a standing position. When the dog sits, mark "YES" then reveal an empty hand. Next treat from the other hand. This weans him off the treat bribe and is known as DELAYED REWARD.

Note: The empty hand and moment of hesitation (delay) keeps a dog guessing and engaged in the command. I call this "becoming a magician for your dog." (It's a trainer's sleight of hand trick, borrowed from magicians.)

6. This time while doing step 1, change the hand into a fist and place it over the dog's head. Gradually increase the distance between your hand and his head. The object is to create a recognizable hand gesture to represent SIT while fading out the food lure.

7. Next, move to a different location in your home and repeat steps 1–4 in a standing position. This teaches a dog to generalize SIT to different areas.

8. Continue to practice SIT in a variety of locations and situations. Be

With self-assured leadership, Desmond commands Ollie into SIT and DOWN.

sure to offer occasional rewards in order to remove the bribe expectation. Include JACKPOT REWARDS (p. 21) for faster SITs. Dogs learn to be attentive, even offering SIT in anticipation of the next JACKPOT.

FEATURED TRAINING TECHNIQUE: DOWN

Quick Description: DOWN

DOWN is a foundation command that places a dog in a submissive position. It's a helpful command at the vet's office, especially in the waiting room with other pets when an owner needs greater control of his dog.

DOWN curbs exuberant canine-greeters and establishes the groundwork for tricks such as roll over, dead dog and army crawl.

DOWN can allay the fears of small children who tend to feel overwhelmed by dogs.

DOWN Steps

1. Start by placing a dog in SIT, then get down on one knee in front of him with a piece of food in your closed fist. Next let him smell the treat.
2. As he sniffs the treat slowly lure his nose toward the ground with a pointed finger to provide a visual cue. Stay close to his chest and body to secure limited movement.
3. You may need to slide your index finger toward the dog's chest and lead his nose to the floor. Then slowly move your index finger to-

ward yourself. This encourages a dog to slide from a SIT into a DOWN position.

4. Once the dog goes into a DOWN position immediately use the marker signal "YES" and treat and praise.

5. Repeat steps 1–4 until DOWN has become a reliable behavior for ten repetitions. Be sure to keep your index finger (physical cue) pointed to the floor the entire time.

6. Next repeat steps 1–4 while slowly changing your body position from kneeling to standing. Be consistent with the luring motion during the transition from kneeling to standing.

7. In the standing position, start DELAYED REWARD (p. 30) while continuing to work on the DOWN command. Do this for ten repetitions, then take a break. End on a JACKPOT and remember to release your dog from the command.

8. Next repeat steps 1–4 while standing (not kneeling) in five other locations. Add in JACKPOT REWARDS for each new location to motivate a dog to do faster DOWNS. Do this for ten repetitions.

Note: DOWN is a command where shaping can apply. If a dog hesitates to go all the way DOWN but goes halfway (front elbows bent), then mark that position with "YES" and treat. Keep him in the game and motivated until he eventually figures out to go all the way DOWN. Pushing or forcing a dog into a DOWN position is a threatening action to a dog. It evokes a fearful response that will set back the training process.

For the more fearful or stubborn pooch, try a different tactic to accomplish the DOWN command. Sit on the floor and raise your knees slightly as though you are making a tunnel for your dog to go under. Next put a treat under the slightly raised knees and lure the dog to the treat. This usually entices the dog to bend down to sniff the treat and then plop DOWN. Mark "YES" and treat. Repeat five to ten times.

Keep in mind that there could possibly be a medical reason (e.g., arthritis or age) for a dog's inability to do a command. In a yoga class, not all students are able to get into every position for a variety of reasons.

SAY WHAT?

There's an emotional component to cooperation training. It's not about barking out commands. It's about adjusting training techniques to be compatible with your dog's needs. Ollie is a social magnet driven by his workaholic party-animal canine-ality. He loves to socialize. We taught SIT and DOWN to mean *"Hi"* and *"How are you?,"* curbing his unwanted behavior while keeping Ollie motivated, focused and engaged in training. It was fun for him to "learn" while earning opportunities to do things he enjoys.

Ollie, the canine mayor of Greenwich Village, kept his social life current with polite "meet and greets." Desmond and Andrew were no longer being pulled in ten directions at once. Ollie's behavior was managed and turned into a reliable habit. He knew what was expected of him. In order to say *"Hi"* and socialize, he had to be responsive to the SIT command. DOWN was for the "conversational" greetings Ollie enjoyed. SIT and DOWN commands were well-behaved greetings cultivated to match Ollie's need to work and have fun. His good behavior turned into reflexive cooperative responses.

"Ollie got me to be able to deal with people better. Practicing SIT and DOWN meant I ended up stopping and talking and engaging with the folks Ollie needed to say 'Hi' and 'How are you?' to," said Desmond.

"His high-maintenance behavior became manageable and cooperative. The commands rechanneled his behavior, conforming perfectly to his canine-ality needs. I discovered who my dog was to me and who I was to him. The logic behind cooperation training connected with my methodical personality. It placed the focus on building the bond while training your dog, which makes sense."

OWNER COMPLIANCE

I often check in with owners to chart progress, assist with any setbacks and deal with new issues. Cooperation training is an evolving and dynamic process that is meant to be flexible. It encourages owners to tweak training techniques to stay current with their dogs' level of learning and needs. Ollie's a herding dog passionate about working. Australian cattle dogs are an active breed that should have ample physical and mental exercise. They need firm leadership, and they must have outlets for their high-energy genetics. I suggested Desmond and Andrew find a person to run with Ollie. This activity would appeal to his workaholic canine-ality and resolve his pent-up vitality. Outside, there'd also be lots of socializing opportunities to satisfy the needs of their party-animal pooch. When I suggested a running partner for Ollie, I never imagined Desmond taking on that job. I assumed they'd hire someone. The self-described curmudgeon had to buy running shoes and attire. He didn't just leave his comfort zone, he ran out of it!

"I didn't want somebody else running with him. I wouldn't have felt comfortable with that," said Desmond. "Okay, so he needs to run, which means we're going to run, was my attitude. I thought I would hate it. Turns out I don't. When we're running you can see that he's having such a good time. I have to all-out run, not jog, because I'm not going to hold him back from what he's there to do. I love it when Ollie gets that look on his face as though he's so happy we're running together. That makes me feel so good."

Owner compliance is a big hurdle to overcome in training. Training tools exist, but if they're not applied, results won't be achieved. My methodology is to create the best possible relationship between you and your dog. Understanding and providing solutions to doggy dynamics is about learning new tricks and developing better communication in order to deepen and enrich the connection between owner and dog.

MEET CHUCK

Chuck has an altogether different canine-ality from Ollie's. The following story is how his owners discovered training techniques that best matched his methodical thinker/sensitive soul and fit in with their lifestyle.

"Chuck was the first dog I saw at the shelter," said Glenn. "I pointed him out to Irene but she mistakenly thought I meant another dog. We then looked at every potential adoptee in the place before I asked again about Chuck. 'You want a pit bull?' That's when I realized she didn't see him. He was cowering in the corner, obscured from her view. We went

INTRIGUING MATCHUPS
Canine-alities

- **GLENN: Workaholic & Party Animal**—He's the worker that's exuberant about what he's doing.
- **IRENE: Methodical Thinker**—She takes it all in, commits to her decisions and is passionate about her family.
- **CHUCK: Methodical Thinker with the soul of a Sensitive Artist.** Training needs to focus on expanding his threshold of tolerance. Engaging him in the training process will build his confidence and set him up for success.

back for another look and this time he came over. He was glassy-eyed and traumatized and he leaned up against us. He was exhausted. Chuck had a lost expression, as though he had no idea what the heck was going on."

Chuck's owners signed up for puppy classes and hired a trainer recommended by the ASPCA. "The first two weeks were tough," said Glenn. "We wondered what we had gotten ourselves into. He was possibly five or six months old, snapping at us, afraid of the dark and generally a total basket case." The first thing the trainer did was establish a foundation for Chuck's basic obedience commands, which, coupled with the owners' compassion and patience, turned a shell-shocked adolescent pup into an affectionate dog. Yet the dog's ever-present protective and territorial behavior still concerned the owners.

During his initial training sessions, Chuck seemed unsure how he should respond, and he consistently shut down. "Halfway through his tenth lesson, Chuck completely broke down and started shaking. It was like he was terrified of the trainer." She finally gave up and told the couple, "He's just one of those dogs. Not very workable."

INTUITIVE OWNERS

For the next two years, Chuck received no formal dog training. His owners provided plenty of love and even canine-homeschooling to establish a consistent routine. The blended personalities of Glenn and Irene nurtured a respectful and trusting human-canine bond that helped manage Chuck's unwanted behavior. However, their intelligent, committed and enthusiastic approach was complicated by the demands of our fast-paced twenty-first-century lifestyles, a common reality for all owners.

Chuck's protective and territorial issues did improve, though they were not fully resolved. Glenn and Irene could only work with him for short spans of time. There was always a point where the sensitive artist would shut down and seek solace in a corner, or regroup in the comfort of his bed. I was able to clearly see that we needed to work on Chuck's threshold of tolerance. It needed to be expanded. This sensitive artist reacted to fear and discomfort at home by retreating and turning in. Outdoors, when Chuck's threshold of tolerance was challenged he'd lunge on leash at dogs and certain strangers. His behavior was becoming unmanageable for his owners.

> Training sessions should be kept to five- to fifteen-minute intervals. This avoids working a dog past his behavioral breaking point (threshold of tolerance). Always end on a good note with a jackpot of treats and lots of praise.

AFFIRMING SECOND OPINION

Glenn and Irene didn't try to push Chuck beyond his limits. In a different home or environment, growling and other aggressive or defensive behavior generally intensifies in this type of dog. This was the case with Chuck. Though intuitive, these owners needed to find a better solution to free up their time. After two years of homeschooling, they contacted me seeking a second opinion from a trainer.

"It's like when you go to a doctor and the first one says, 'I don't know what it is,' and the second one comes up with a different diagnosis that you connect with. The analysis Kate provided was affirming to us," said Glenn. The first trainer gave Chuck's owners a solid foundation for basic obedience. Overlooked was Chuck's canine-ality.

Methodical Thinker. That was my first impression of Chuck, an eighty-pound Greater Swiss Mountain coonhound mix. However, he had the soul of a sensitive artist.

DOG DOCTOR

LOOK-AT-ME and TOUCH TARGET commands are my diagnostic tools. I use both of these Pay Attention commands the same way a doctor uses a stethoscope. They give me the ability to read a dog's behavioral pulse by concentrating on his responses and reactivity, using a non-evasive, nonthreatening method. In my first session with Chuck, I noticed that he paused before responding to either of those commands. I could see him thinking and considering what was being asked of him. That's what led me to determine he was a methodical thinker. Chuck's threshold of tolerance is limited and fragile. He was shutting down because his root canine-ality is that of a sensitive artist.

NEWBORN REALITIES

Canine-ality types, like the canine drives, provide owners with targeted insight into better understanding their dogs. Chuck is reserved and thinks before responding to a command, though his sensitive artist side has the tendency to become overwhelmed. Glenn, a workaholic–party animal, runs his business and doesn't always have the time he'd like to devote to Chuck's training needs. Irene, a methodical thinker, is thoughtful and passionate, and at the time I met her, she was pregnant. With a baby on the way, Chuck's unwanted behaviors needed to be resolved.

The couple understood that his threatening behavior would likely be exacerbated by the addition of a newborn, a stroller and other baby-related issues. Consequently, their household, lifestyle and time management would be challenged. It was time to shift gears in their approach to working with Chuck. This couple committed to setting up their dog for success. Chuck's sense of being overwhelmed required an appealing training technique that would turn him on. Engaging him in the process would not only modify unwanted behaviors, but would build up his confidence and self-esteem.

TRAINING TECHNIQUES SPECIFIC TO CHUCK

Having identified Chuck's canine-ality, I explained to the owners that they needed to be decisive when giving commands and that correcting him would carry a great deal of meaning. They also needed to keep in mind that his sensitivity trait would be reactive to their tone of voice and to their facial expressions and body language. All this worked in their favor with the lunging and barking because, at heart, Chuck wanted to get it right. A firm "NO" or "LEAVE IT" command (telling the dog what not to do) followed by a TOUCH TARGET redirect (telling the dog what to do) in Chuck's case quickly resolved what the owners originally called me in for.

> When giving commands be firm but don't bark out orders. Avoid repeating commands and don't make them sound like you're asking a question.

Plenty of owners complain about lunging and barking and I work with them to resolve those issues. However, it's important that they understand the root cause of the problem. Lasting change in canine behavior is secured by doing more than just fixing the symptoms (barking, lunging, growling). While Chuck's owners' original concern was lunging and barking, that wasn't the only problem. Their sensitive artist was also shutting down during training sessions.

It was also necessary to turn down Chuck's pack drive while turning on his prey drive. I wanted to shift him away from being a Velcro dog that followed his owners everywhere, especially because a baby was soon to enter the picture and someone else would be vying for his owners' attentions. A tiny infant becoming the focal point of the household would impact everyone, including Chuck. Now was the time for the owners' firstborn to regain his confidence and find his independence. This family needed to be prepared and equipped for the new realities soon to take place in their household.

FEATURED TRAINING TECHNIQUE: GO FIND IT

Quick Description: GO FIND IT

The GO FIND IT command helps dogs understand that paying attention to owners is fun and rewarding.

BENEFITS: It turns on dogs' primary instincts and connects them back to what they were bred to do, such as hunt, forage and chase.

EXERCISE, EXERCISE and EXERCISE is another perk linked with this command. For those dogs that don't get enough outdoor time, GO FIND IT keeps them from becoming stir-crazy indoors on rainy or snowy days.

For Velcro dogs (dogs that follow owners everywhere), GO FIND IT is a stress reliever for both them and their owners. This technique helps pooches gradually build up their confidence and autonomy. GO FIND IT can also be helpful for dogs with separation anxiety issues.

GOAL: Being innovative and having fun with the training.

GO FIND IT Steps

1. Start with LOOK-AT-ME or TOUCH TARGET to ensure the dog's attention is on you by using a high-value treat—the human equivalent of a $100 bill. Note: For dogs motivated by toys over food, make the proper substitution.

2. Toss the treat three feet away with a pointed arm to provide directional guidance. This will motivate the dog to run off and look for the food with his nose. Repeat this five to ten times, and keep increasing the distance until your dog gets the idea.

3. Once the dog is getting the concept reliably, command with the verbal cue "GO FIND IT." As the dog runs off, wait two seconds. Then without him noticing, quickly toss treats over his head a good distance (DELAYED REWARD). Think of it as your dog having a job to do first before he gets paid. He must GO FIND IT to be rewarded.

4. Alternatively, play this game by putting the dog in another room or a crate, then hide the treats or toys around the home. Let the dog out and command, "GO FIND IT." When he finds the individual treat or toy, offer praise.

5. Repeat this exercise in at least five to ten different locations inside and outside your home and neighborhood. Outside, GO FIND IT can be modified using short distances in order to keep a dog's focus away from unwanted distractions.

Note: Tossing the treats or toys in a varied pattern keeps dogs in the game of playing GO FIND IT. I have found that establishing a command for this inbred instinct can help stop unwanted outdoor scavenging. Dogs learn that scavenging and foraging happen when their owners give the cue for it.

GO FIND IT plays to a dog's natural instincts. The command places it on cue.

> GO FIND IT is mentally stimulating for dogs. It keeps them more attentive to their owners' commands.

AIN'T NOTHING LIKE A HOUND DOG

The GO FIND IT training technique is what got Chuck reengaged in using his canine senses of sight, smell, sound, taste and touch. This fun command technique is a mental, problem-solving game that appealed to his methodical-thinking side. I knew Chuck would easily succeed with GO FIND IT and even tap into his sensitive artist trait to perform it. His owners, a willing, captive audience, would provide ample reinforcement praise to reward his behavior. Chuck would begin to trust himself more as his threshold of tolerance expanded.

> I call my canine clients that master GO FIND IT skills "semi-professional search-and-rescue dogs." Bet you didn't realize your Maltese was capable of being more than just so darn cute.

FUN FACTOR

The GO-FIND-IT command brought out Chuck's Scooby-Doo "Gotta-do" workaholic scramble-slide run. His back legs would cartoonbackpedal like propellers, followed by a slide across the floor. It was hysterical and a departure from his methodical-sensitive artist canine-ality. It got him out of his head while expanding his threshold.

"Canine-alities gave us the freedom to be flexible and innovative with our training techniques. The layered—instead of one-way—approach matched up all of our 'alities'—workaholic, party animal, methodical thinker and sensitive artist. His threshold of tolerance was expanded and so was ours! Taking him to day care and hiring dog walkers additionally fostered Chuck's party-boy side," said Glenn.

PRACTICALITIES

Dogs are often chosen by looks, size and perceived canine-alities. Life-styles, households and budgets shouldn't be overlooked when consider-ing your relationship with your dog. Dogs are remarkable at adapting to everything around them, but they do need to know what's expected of them. Consider your lifestyle, household makeup and finances when making the commitment to owning a dog and being responsible for his welfare. Proper diet, exercise, socializing, grooming, training, playtime, mental stimulation, bathroom necessities and medical care will all be needed.

Whether you live in a house, an apartment, in multiple dwellings or a dormitory, a dog must be introduced to the setting and what's associated with it, including what's required and expected of him in those locations. Bond with your dog during training and make the connection. The train-ing focus should go beyond mastering basic obedience commands. It's about your connection to your dog.

Puppyhood: Speculation or Investment?

The responsibilities and upheavals that arise when a puppy enters a household are both exciting and daunting. The goal of my cooperation methodology is to help make sure you have made a wise investment in your pup's training, not a wild speculation. You've made a big commitment. There's a lot of work ahead to help him make a successful transition into your lifestyle. Owners can be surprised at how much time and energy is required. Be patient while establishing a connection of calm authority with your puppy. The goal is to encourage, engage and motivate him to be responsive to commands. Puppies need you to nurture them and provide leadership and guidance.

A puppy enters a home having left his family, companions and primary teachers. Everything familiar to the puppy has been stripped away. Between eight and sixteen weeks of age is one of the most impressionable times in a pup's life. It's important for owners to realize that their pup's education has been abruptly interrupted and needs to be reinstated right away.

The interactions that take place with mother and siblings within the whelping pen are more than just play. Survival skills are being taught. The canine drives of pack, prey, flight and fight are being honed. Hierarchy, boundaries, manners, bite inhibition and social aptitude are all part of the crucial interplay that at a cursory glance seems random, adorable and purposeless. However, that isn't the case.

If you're an owner who got a late start with training, or who has rescued an older dog, or if you are fostering or doing in-home housesitting for a relative or friend, this chapter will also help you. The optimal learning window may have passed, but it's never over. Improvements can be made to socializing skills, bite inhibition and housebreaking behaviors. Keep in mind while reading that training may require more time and pa-

Puppies aren't born knowing how to fit into our lives, and the hellion Huckleberry was no exception.

tience because most dogs entering an unfamiliar home or setting will be overwhelmed.

THE PUP NAMED "NO"

"No" was four and a half months old when I became his trainer. This English cocker spaniel was living with a family of four plus a nanny. Confusion ran rampant. No took it all in stride, bouncing off walls and doing laps around the apartment as if he were training for a marathon. He also happily took to the game of chase, which was often initiated by family members repeatedly calling his name while racing toward him. The fanfare of this "Nooo" activity was terrific fun for No.

Every puppy loves a good game of chase. It combines all of the instinctive drives of prey, fight, flight and pack. It also elicits puppy antics such as strategic maneuvering, barreling, busting through obstacles and jumping on tables. No was sharpening his action-hero moves, which were becoming more defined every time he tore through the living room. His in-it-to-win expression expertly taunted pursuers with an unmistakable "COME GET ME" grimace. It was hard to ignore his panting, head cocking at just the right angle and hindquarters shifting like a rodeo bull. Yes, he was downright incorrigible and adorable.

The early stages of raising a puppy come with mixed feelings. Owners often go through a phase of renaming their puppy "No." "No," also known as Huckleberry, wasn't a bad puppy. He was normal, healthy and athletic. From his perspective, adaptation to his new family and surroundings was going great. For No and other "No"-named pups, educational needs were being overlooked. No didn't have his mother and littermates to provide corrections. His impulsive behavior was going unchecked.

OWNER ASSESSMENT

"We decided on an English cocker spaniel for a few reasons," said Allison. "First, the breed had to be good with children. Second, my husband wanted a hunting dog, one with a lively temperament. Finally, size was important—not too big or too small. Huckleberry didn't disappoint us." Huckleberry's owners decided on a specific breed based on generalized temperament and size traits. An English cocker spaniel belonging to a member of their hunting club sealed the deal. "He was lovely with our kids. Just the kind of dog we were looking for." They contacted the same breeder and were told that a litter would be available soon.

Huckleberry's family did a good job assessing what type of dog they wanted for their household. They even contacted a veterinarian, who provided them with my business card. "I knew we would need a trainer," said Allison. "My nine-year-old daughter, Helen, and seven-year-old son, Harry, had both wanted to get a puppy for a long time. Conveying to children all that's required to take care of a dog can feel like nagging. I didn't want to be in that position. When I first spoke with Kate, she encouraged us as a family to enroll in puppy class."

Owner assessments should also include financial resources, time availability, lifestyle conditions and the everyday function of the household. To keep consistency in training, identify the individuals who will be part of your pet's inner circle and define their roles. For example, relatives, neighbors, dog walkers and live-in help will be interacting with and influencing your puppy. Inform them of the training protocol established for your pup and ask them to use the same guidelines. With delivery people, groomers, shopkeepers and even strangers excited to meet your puppy, be proactive in a friendly fashion that makes them an extension of your training team. No one will take offense when an owner asks others for help reinforcing canine manners. And don't forget to factor into the evaluation the other issues addressed in chapters 3 (canine drives) and 4 (canine-alities).

PUPPY SUPPORT GROUP

Puppies aren't born knowing how to fit into our lives. They enter a home with a heartbeat, irresistible puppy breath and a pink tongue. As you watch your puppy wander around the house with his nose to the ground, you feel good. He's making himself comfortable, you think, and then he sniffs, circles and piddles on the floor. No worries, he's just nervous; things are new to him. But before you finish wiping up that mess, he poops. Okay, to be expected. Then suddenly he takes off at Tasmanian devil speed, grabbing the remote control or other handy objects such as shoes, clothing or wiring. When confronted, he growls at you. By now you're starting to wake up to the fact that he's not settling in, he's destroying everything in sight, including your life.

Puppies and owners find themselves confronted with changes and adjustments that are both physical and mental. Life is irrevocably, and sometimes drastically, modified when a scruff of fur is welcomed into the family. Emotions from big love to frustration—as well as exhaustion and confusion—intensify. Owners often have conflicting feelings during the puppy phase, ages six to sixteen weeks: *Why did I get a puppy?* or *Why didn't I get a puppy sooner?*

My puppy classes place less emphasis on a strict curriculum and more on what dog owners are dealing with "right now," at the "my wit's end" moment. The basics include housetraining, obedience, bite inhibition and walking on-leash. The gap between owners and new puppies has to be bridged.

My puppy class uses a format similar to a support group. Owners and pups gather in a circle and talk about their dog-parenting issues. The key is to deal with problems and new developments as they arise. Owners find that they are not alone because they are part of an understanding and nurturing group sharing similar challenges, such as: "He barks until he gets stuff." Or "There's something wrong with my puppy—she never uses her pee pad." Or "My dog is convinced that I'm his chew toy." Let's break down some of the most common issues to explain them from a pup's perspective.

Problem: The dog barks until he gets stuff. Most likely he's getting stuff, and that's rewarding to him.

Puppy: *"It took me about a day or two to train my owner. Then he realized bark-bark-bark means give me whatever I demand. Hey, Kate, is there a faster way to train humans?"*

Owner solution: Make an interruptive "EH-EH" sound or clap your hands. This disrupts his barking. Then wait for him to be quiet. Once you capture that moment of silence, reward him with praise and treats.

Problem: The puppy uses the shower stall instead of her pee pad. Could it be a medical condition? Let's ask the owner a few questions:

- Is she crate-trained? "No."
- So she has free roam of the house? "Yes."
- Is water and food available for her at all times? "Yes."
- And her energy and behavior are otherwise normal? "She's perfectly healthy."
- Is the door to your bathroom left open? Owners tend to pause before responding, "Yes."

Puppy: *"I'm a secret pee-er. Privacy matters. I've chosen a loo area that makes perfect sense and apparently was designed for this purpose—the shower stall."*

Owner solution: The evidence: free rein of the home (access to shower stall), availability of food and water at her whim, lack of supervision and a healthy, playful pup. Why did I ask about the bathroom door being left open? This secret pee-er sniffs out drains, choosing to do her business in the shower stall.

Start with a containment area, crate training and 100 percent supervision! Water and food should not be available at all times. Schedule all meals, treats and water. Knowing what goes in helps to predict what will come out. After naps and within a short span of time after finishing a meal or drinking water, a puppy will likely need to relieve herself. Take her to the designated elimination spot when she wakes up. Wait five to ten minutes after food and water and then provide her with another bathroom break opportunity. (See chapter 6 for more on housetraining.)

Problem: The owner is a chew toy in disguise.

Puppy: *"Dude—you know you like it. Admit to the trainer that whenever I chew on you, you allow it so I keep at it. Then you want to play chase and whatever. I like that game, too."*

Owner Solution: The new game is you say, "OUCH," and turn or walk away. Play aloof and ignore. React less and redirect the pup's attention to items that are appropriate chew toys. (See bite inhibition and the three-stage process of controlling a dog's mouth later in this chapter.)

SOCIALIZING 101

The best way to give your puppy a head start is through supervised and controlled socialization, and good old common sense. Since pups are social creatures, avoid too much isolation. Emphasizing the shaping and development of positive coping skills keeps a pup responding to new situations and circumstances without being fearful or exercising too much caution. Early exposure and socialization is the best way to prevent behavioral problems in dogs.

Puppies have a natural immunity to most common diseases as a result of the antibodies passed on from nursing. However, it's important to exercise caution prior to full vaccination. I recommend puppy socialization classes and managed playgroups to get pups and owners out and about. Until fully vaccinated, however, avoid dog runs. Instead sit outside a dog park so your puppy becomes used to the excitement and noises they'll soon be a part of.

If a pup has only one playmate, goes out only twice a day, has little interaction with other dogs or people and is more or less confined to the home, he's not properly socialized. He's missing the opportunity to develop healthy coping and social skills that will prepare him to handle potential canine stressors. Take my five-year-old son, for example. Do I want him to have only one friend? Wouldn't he be better off having multiple friends to play with? If he isn't exposed to other cultures or ethnicities, or if he fails to get out and about in the world, will he be equipped to handle the surprises life tosses his way? A puppy needs the same type of learning experiences.

Keeping a puppy cut off from sights, sounds, smells, people, healthy dogs and a host of other realities sets that dog up for failure. The socialization of puppies, rescues and, in general, all dogs is of paramount importance. It should begin right away and continue for the life of the dog.

While puppies are within their series of vaccination shots, avoid taking them to off-leash dog parks and stay away from puddles of old water and any situation that might present a health risk.

SEVEN DAYS OF DISCOVERY

Puppyhood doesn't last forever. When puppies enter our homes ready to explore, interpret and react to their surroundings, everything is new. Introducing a pup to new people, places, sounds, tastes, smells and objects is a principle of cooperation dog training. What I like to call "Seven Days of Discovery" is a critical stage of development. It is a fun, user-friendly concept designed to build lasting trust, confidence and reliability in canine behavior. It's also crafted to enhance the bond between owners and pups while creating those precious first-ever moments.

7 DAYS OF DISCOVERY
Foundation Exposures

- PEOPLE
- SURFACES
- OBJECTS
- LOCATIONS
- SOUNDS
- CHALLENGES
- DINING EXPERIENCES

7 DAYS, 3X A DAY
(morning, afternoon & evening) in each of the categories will add up to almost

150 FOUNDATION EXPOSURES

© Yvonne Conza

For one week, three times a day (morning, afternoon and evening), expose your puppy to one of each of the following:

- People—infant, senior, bearded male, tall woman, someone walking with a cane, toddler, teen.
- Surfaces—grass, concrete, carpet, linoleum, wood, metal grates, sand.
- Objects—ball, Frisbee, hairbrush, nail clippers, hammer, umbrella, bowl.
- Locations—backyard, basement, car, hallway, vet's office, groomer, park.
- Sounds—hair dryer, vacuum cleaner, fax machine, doors opening and closing, squeaky toys, doorbell, sirens.

- Challenges—kids on skateboards, going up and down stairs, walking past homeless people, people wanting to pet and handle him, toddlers chasing, going through narrow hallways, riding in an elevator.
- Dining Experiences—in crate, living room, kitchen, outdoors, hand-feeding, inside portable travel bag, at doggy day care.

Be sure to make all introductions with an upbeat, enthusiastic tone while maintaining a relaxed body position. Have yummy high-value treats on hand during the Seven Days of Discovery activities to reinforce a "good things happen" vibe in new and unfamiliar settings, situations and encounters. It's all about building the pup's confidence. In seven days, a pup can easily be introduced to almost 150 situations and experiences. The user-friendly approach encourages you to maintain the discovery phase momentum for the rest of your dog's life, not just for seven days. Take note of reactions and see if you can identify the following:

- Fearful
- Timid
- Aggressive
- Excited
- Cautious
- Withdrawn
- Happy
- Eager
- Anxious
- Surprised
- Anticipating
- Inquisitive
- Overwhelmed

- Friendly
- Affectionate
- Calm
- Content
- Relaxed

Documenting the pup's reactions as they occur helps you and anyone else working with your dog better understand and therefore resolve any behavioral challenges. By focusing on who your dog is and observing how he reacts to things, you are an active participant in the training process. The interaction creates yet another rewarding layer of bonding between you and your dog.

> Puppies need to be handled by as many people as possible. Their paws, ears and tails should be gently rubbed and massaged. This will make visits to the vet, groomer and others less stressful. Try using an infant finger brush to get a pup used to having his teeth brushed and examined.

Seven Days of Discovery is all about socializing and habituating your puppy to his surroundings. Chapter 7 is devoted entirely to this topic. Socialization matters not only for puppies; rescue, senior and medically challenged dogs also need hobnobbing. It's key to integrate scheduled socializing soirees as early as possible and to maintain them for the lifetime of your dog. A well-behaved pup will be welcomed almost everywhere. Think of socialization as social currency. Make your dog and yourself wealthy in the mixing and mingling of life!

A FEW PUPPY FIRSTS:
NAME, ID AND PREP LIST

Picking a name for a puppy is not only necessary, it's personal. It's the beginning of the owner's attachment to the puppy and the introduction to his training. Choose a name that has significance and one that everyone in the family will have no problem relating to or saying in public.

When working with puppies, owners need to be patient
and consistent with their training techniques.

Nicknames such as Pooper, Lover or Big Butt may seem funny and descriptive, but on the street can elicit unwanted and unflattering attention. Other names to avoid are those that could in any way be confused with commands, such as Fetch.

Should it be a one- or two-syllable name? My experience tends to favor the latter. (Going beyond two syllables is not recommended.) The perfect name is one with which both ends of the leash can have a positive association. It can be imaginative, fun and distinctive. An ID tag is essential, so be sure to get one right away. Make sure the information is readable and your contact information is up-to-date.

Astro, Bison, Cupid, Duchess, Elvis, Freckles, Gatsby, Harley, Iggy, Joey, Karma, Lady, Murphy, Nutmeg, Otto, Peanut, Queeny, Ragtime, Scamper, Tango, Ulla, Vida, Willow, X-ray, Yoshi, Zulu
Note: When making a correction, avoid using your dog's name. Instead say "NO" or use an interruptive noise like "EH–EH."

PREP LIST CHEAT SHEET

Canine Nursery and Other Supplies

- A crate and/or playpen (if you don't go with both, you'll need baby gates to create a proper containment area).
- Pet-specific cleaners like Nature's Miracle (an enzymatic cleaner used to remove the scent of stool and urine) and Grannick's Bitter Apple (a chew-deterrent solution that can also be used on hot spots). Avoid substituting inferior products for quality brands like these.
- Other essentials such as paw wipes, wee-wee pads, nail file, soft finger toothbrush, ear and eye cleaners.

Choosing a Veterinarian

Plan ahead and don't wait until there's a problem. Start by asking for recommendations from dog owner friends, breeders, shelter workers and groomers. Confirm affiliation with the American Animal Hospital Association. Schedule a brief interview with the veterinarian and members of the vet's staff and tour the facility. (See chapter 10, "Health: Mind, Body and Wag.")

Members of Pup's Team

If your daily schedule leaves you with limited time, assemble a support staff that includes friends, neighbors, doorman, professional dog sitters, walkers and doggy day care.

Preschool

Enroll in a puppy class and arrange for playdates. Think of it as preparing your dog to face the world. Make sure there's plenty of mental and physical stimulation for the little guy. "Exercise, exercise, exercise and socialize" should be the motto for puppyhood—and for the lifespan of your dog.

Canine Guardian Style

Do you want a four-pound bundle of fur calling the shots in your household? Take charge and adhere to routines and housetraining schedules. Teaching a pup what is desired and expected is crucial in the early stages of puppyhood. Consider hiring a trainer for a house call to assist with identifying good leadership skills best suited for both ends of the leash.

Toys

- Kong—hollow pear-shaped natural rubber toy made to be stuffed with treats or a filling that will occupy a dog's interest for hours.

- Nylabones—hard-rubber, non-digestible chew bone that cleans teeth and helps prevent tartar buildup.
- Interactive toys. I really like the fun, interactive Busy Buddy treat dispensers, especially the Twist 'n Treat models by Premier Pet Products.
- Stuffless toys by Premier Pet Products.

Food

- Merrick
- Wellness
- Honest Kitchen
- Dogswell Vitality
- Now! Grain Free
- Home-cooked

Treats and Chews

- Easy-to-digest chew sticks such as bully sticks and spiral Flossies
- Natural Balance
- Stella & Chewy's
- Low-fat string cheese

Equipment

- Lightweight collar with ID tags (tags can come off inside your home but must be on whenever outdoors or in unfamiliar settings). Note: Take off collar and tags when a pup is in the containment area or inside his crate. This prevents tags from getting caught between crate wires and prevents a pup from chewing on them.

- SENSE-ation No-Pull Harness or Easy Walk Harness (both are designed to lead the movement of a pup's walk from the chest and prevent a dog from pulling his owners. This equipment is for walking purposes only and shouldn't be worn around the house or during playtime.)

HANDLING THE SITUATION

Puppies don't come out of the womb knowing how to accept being handled. They have to be taught and desensitized to it. This takes time and patience. Familiarizing a pup with his collar and leash doesn't have to be intimidating. In fact, if you have children, this can be a terrific opportunity to instill respectful handling of the newest family member. It's also about understanding the simple act of learning how to wait while conditioning and reinforcing self-control for "No" pups like Huckleberry.

Chasing Huckleberry was not a way for Helen and Harry to get a collar and leash on their puppy. However, by adding TOUCH, a one-syllable command approach to training, with stillness and a confident, decisive tone of voice, a new game was in play. Huckleberry was intrigued and lured by the command. He liked learning a fun new game that involved marking and rewarding desired behavior. Helen and Harry felt empowered by this leadership technique of training that uses motivation, not force. Handling the situation in a cooperative manner built trust and connection at both ends of the leash. It also made it easier to get a collar and leash on Huckleberry.

FEATURED TRAINING TECHNIQUE: COLLAR AND LEASH

Quick Description: Collar and Leash

Getting a puppy familiar with a collar is an important part of the training process. All dogs need walks, even those country pooches that head into town for errands or to visit the farmers' market with their owners.

Fit: There should be room to snugly slide one finger between the collar and the pup's neck. Be certain the collar is not loose enough to easily pull over the dog's head.

Goal: The purpose is to gain a pup's cooperation when introducing the collar or harness while he's pulling away, cringing or nipping.

Collar and Leash Steps

1. Use a lightweight collar and leash and start by introducing them inside your home. Washable nylon fabrics and those with easy snap-on clasps are recommended.

2. Attach the collar or harness just before feeding to make a positive association with the equipment. Fido: *"Collar on and food is served. Nice concept!"*

   Note: It takes a little longer to put on a harness. To reduce a puppy's frustration and resistance, distract him. Offer him a bully stick or try filling a Kong with some yummy food like cream cheese while clasping the harness on. This helps reduce a puppy's desire to nip at you while you make the adjustments.

3. It's normal to expect some initial pawing at the collar. If this happens, redirect the pup's attention using a chew stick or toy.

4. Attach the leash and practice walking around your home with your pup. If he pulls you or resists, simply stop and wait for him to calm down. Stay neutral and don't overreact if he pulls. Instead, wait for him to return to a composed state. When he relaxes, capture that moment of calm by giving him a treat, praise or a toy. This teaches and reinforces that when he is calm and amiable, with leash and collar on, good things happen. Then proceed to walk him with the leash on.

5. Practice during feedings and then progress to working with the equipment during playtime. It's important to familiarize him with the collar and leash throughout the day for the first week.

PUPPYSCAPING

On my first visit, No was free to roam the house. He delighted in showing me his canine athletic skills, which included high dives from the sofa and leaps onto the dining room table. I noted that his food and water bowls were refilled regularly—never empty. This dog had quite a life and seemed to accept "No" and versions of "Noooo" as his name. Did I mention that he wasn't housebroken?

Generally when there's a housetraining problem, there's no proper setup. In other words, the home needs a containment area—a space that can be cordoned off with an exercise pen. It should be located away from entryways and areas of high traffic. The pen should contain a crate with a bed, a wee-wee pad positioned on the perimeter, toys and bowls for food and water.

Puppyscaping is less about design and more about structure. A pup needs to acclimate to his surroundings. A containment area is for the

owner's benefit as well as the puppy's. It provides the ability to supervise, control and train during the early stages of housetraining, and it
helps with mouthing issues (bite inhibition). With a lot of space, Huckleberry was a wild man. There was no way to control his behavioral impulses. Peeing indoors wasn't right or wrong for him. How would he
know? No boundaries had ever been established. Abundant water and
food only added to the housetraining dilemma since what goes in must
come out.

Containment Area: Choose a low-traffic area that's away from entryways. This can be tricky with limited space. Gating an area in the kitchen
or bathroom might suffice. The key is to find a place that's conducive to
the puppy easily settling down.

PUPPYSCAPING = CONTAINMENT AREA

- EXERCISE PEN
- CRATE/BED
- WEE-WEE PAD

- CHEW BONES
- STUFFLESS/SQUEAKY TOYS
- BOWLS

Puppy area should always have a rotation of toys such as Kongs, Busy Buddy Twist 'n Treat, soft non-stuffed toys and a hard rubber ball. With interactive puzzle toys, supervision is recommended.

PUPPY PROOFING

Puppy proofing a home is as important as creating a proper containment area for your dog. Loose wires, exposed outlets, decorative ornaments or anything that, if chewed, could splinter and become an intestinal obstruction should be removed or properly contained to avoid risk to your puppy's life. Consider covering furniture and table legs with hard rubber tubing sprayed with Grannick's Bitter Apple for additional "chew" insurance.

To maximize puppy proofing, take the 4-Paw tour. Get down low and view your home from a pooch's perspective. The floor-length curtains may need to be tied back or pulled up. Low cabinets that a paw could open should be properly latched and secured closed. The antique quilt dangling over the bed might have to be removed until housetraining becomes reliable. Rug tassels that can easily resemble a rope chew toy should be folded underneath to avoid potential chewing.

TRAINING TECHNIQUES
SPECIFIC TO
HUCKLEBERRY, AKA "NO"

The first thing we did for Huckleberry was take away his free-roaming pass and create a containment area. Next we implemented a food and water schedule. Finally, all bathroom activity was accounted for on a chart. A housetraining chart can assist owners in becoming Sherlock Canine Holmes detectives capable of discovering a pattern to their dog's bathroom habits. The housetraining chart below is used to provide the clues (timing) that solve most pee and poo mysteries for owners. As trainers like to say, "He who controls the bladder succeeds at housetraining!"

Monday	Water / Food	Routine / Things to do	Toy Rotation	Pee	Poop	Accident
6:30 am	Food #1, Water #1	Out for a walk or go to pad		1x	1x	
7:30 am	Water #2	Free supervised time if peed / pooped. Play & some training / fetch. Water then back outside or to pad before leaving for work		1 or 2x		
8:30 am		In containment area, pen / crate while alone	Bully stick, frozen baby carrot and stuffed toy			
11:30 / 12:00pm	Food #2 (if three meals a day) Water #3	Walker or owner comes home. Give water before going outside. Then back in crate / pen		1x	1x	
1:00 - 2:00 pm		Crate / pen while alone	New set of toys give frozen Kong and squeaky			
3:00 pm	Water #4	Walker comes back. Gives water before going outside. Then back in crate / pen	New set of toys, e.g. rope toy, Kong, bully stick	1x		

4:00 pm		Crate / pen while alone					
5:30 / 6:00 pm	Food #2 / 3 Water #5	Walk after food / water			1x	1x	
6:30 - 8:00 pm	Water #6	Great time for playdate / training session. Then a walk and last water					
9:00 pm		Last outing or pad before bed			1x	1x	
9:30 pm		Crate / pen for bedtime	Stuffed toy, ice cube				

"NO" was heard less and less around the home as Huckleberry began to identify more with his actual name. He still got his share of chase and gotcha interplay, but the chaos had been replaced with a calm energy and "naughty dog" was no longer cornered and placed in his crate. Using the GO FIND IT command, canine sports like chase were retooled for Huckleberry. Helen and Harry became coaches teaching Huckleberry

how to curb his impulsive behavior. GO FIND IT was the interactive game with rules and structure that managed his behavior. It was also an activity (command) that honed his prey drive and prepared him to go hunting with his owner.

When Huckleberry got overexcited and jumped on them, Helen and Harry turned their backs on him and stood still (for kids, use imagery and say, "Stand like a tree") while ignoring him. This works because the dog, not wanting to lose their attention,

"Stand like a tree" posture, demonstrated by Helen and Harry, helps to curb a dog from jumping up on people.

would then sit (instead of jumping at them) and wait for them to turn back. The children would then give Huckleberry a treat for the right behavior. It became a motivating and rewarding system teaching Huckleberry patience. He was learning while earning his rightful place in their home and hearts.

> Owners lament that their puppy doesn't seem to know his name. "I say his name ten thousand times a day and get no response." Dogs are like people. If they're not listening, even when you say things over and over, what they've learned to do is ignore you.
>
> Say your pet's name once as you lure him with a treat. Repeat, but only when you have his attention. Be sure to use a positive tone of voice, and when he responds to his name, quickly praise and treat.

MOUTH MANNERS MATTER

Though born without teeth, puppies will have about twenty-eight razor-sharp ones by the time they are eight weeks old. Play biting, mouthing and chewing are normal, not malicious, behaviors. They are his ways of exploring and coming to know his world. However, he needs to be taught the appropriate threshold level and the proper amount of force as it relates to a variety of mouthing scenarios. Owners need to teach pups the difference between gentle play mouthing a human and chewing a bone. TOUCH TARGET is used to inform a dog that his nose—not his mouth—is the primary acceptable and desired tool for dog-human physical interaction.

Puppies need to be taught that chewing and biting chair legs, shoes and owners' body parts aren't welcomed activities. When this behavior occurs, owners must immediately distract and redirect with a lure using treats or toys. Once their focus is gained, pups should be redirected to an appropriate item intended for chewing purposes, such as a bone or peanut-butter-filled Kong. A puppy will start to distinguish between what can and cannot be chewed. Coaching a pup must be done in a consistent, repetitious manner to gain reliable behavior. All training requires repetition, patience and consistency.

A dog that fails to learn mouth manners could become a biter and consequently a legal liability. To avoid injuries (physical, emotional and financial), take the time to work on developing a soft mouth. Hand-feeding is a wonderful bonding experience while teaching your puppy a gentle way to take something from you. If his mouthing for a treat is too forceful, or involves his scalpel-like teeth sinking into you, yell, "OUCH," and turn away. Wait a few seconds then try again. Likely he'll recall his days of nursing from his mother when, if he was too rough, she also got up and walked away.

Hand-feeding is a great method for households with children. It can lower the resource-guarding issues some dogs develop if they instinctively start to feel territorial or threatened. It's essential to establish a firm house rule that informs a puppy that anyone is allowed to be near him while he's eating, without him reacting aggressively. (We discuss the benefits and best techniques of hand-feeding in greater detail in chapter 7, "Tailgating.")

Nipping and biting is dog culture. It's canine conversing and a source of play. Pouncing, stalking, tagging one another (other dogs or an owner) and use of the mouth are all pure dedicated puppy merriment. Professor Sophie understands that sometimes her students will cut up in class. They'll go too far and test boundaries with one another. Occasionally a yelp or whine will erupt and that tells the fellow student that he was too rough and being a bully. If the teaser or intimidator continues to go past the thresholds of others, he'll soon discover that nobody wants to play with him.

My puppy classes are a controlled and supervised canine schoolyard. They give owners and puppies the opportunity to work at and act out new concepts and behaviors in real time and with professional guidance. This book helps with, but does not replace, the live interactions (socialization) that take place in classes between owners and their pups, pups and other pups, and owners and other people's pups. Animal shelters are filled with dogs that, taken too soon from mothers and littermates, or not mentored by owners, lack important developmental canine cultivation. We owe it to them to fill in the learning gaps that were taken from them at eight to ten weeks old, or sadly sometimes even six weeks old.

BITE INHIBITION 101

Sophie, my pug, is an integral part of instilling mouthing and other canine manners in my puppy class. Her hierarchal role as older dog is instinctively understood and generally respected by puppies. That doesn't mean they won't test her, and they do. She then corrects them. As we learned in chapter 1, canine body language that includes sideways glances, licking and body shakes sends a message to another dog.

When a pup crosses a boundary with Professor Sophie, she politely lets him know to knock it off. If he doesn't get the message, she upgrades her canine speak (p. 11) to include her cut-off signals of licking, shake-offs, head turns and body blocks. Still not getting the message? The professor will then take him to the floor in a safe, controlled canine pin-down in front of the entire class.

Professor Sophie covers most of the basics of bite inhibition. The purpose of mouthing manners is to shape and teach a puppy to have a gentle mouth. Training needs to encourage and reinforce that mouthing and

Professor Sophie specializes in teaching
puppies canine manners.

biting humans is not acceptable or tolerated behavior. Chewing is okay when directed at objects designed for this purpose, such as bones or chew toys, or between dogs where the mouthing matchup is understood to be play, not aggression.

Teething Tip: Dip a Kong in chicken stock and then place it in the freezer. When your pup starts teething, redirect his behavior by giving him the frozen chicken-flavored Kong. For a more savory teething tool, take the iced Kong and stuff it with cream cheese or wet food. Frozen baby carrots are also great to use.

Getting angry at a pup that nips at you will not teach him what not to do or what you'd prefer he do. Instead, behavior should be corrected and redirected. Here is a list of three easy steps to take when training for bite inhibition:

1. Start by offering your pup a soft squeaky toy. Let him bite it as hard as he likes and even play a light tug-of-war game with him. Do this for about thirty seconds.

2. Slowly inch your hands to the area where your pup is mouthing the toy. The idea is to set the pup up to accidentally nip your hand. *Be ready for this!* When you feel teeth on your hand, no matter what pressure, immediately yell, "OUCH!" Then take the toy and go behind a closed door for ten to fifteen seconds. Walking away is a reprimand (abandonment training) that is used to inform the pup that, if he uses his teeth, he loses the owner's attention and playtime.

3. Return after fifteen seconds and, using a happy tone, encourage play again with the toy. Some pups will misunderstand that biting the toy was what caused you to leave. Coax him with a soft, enthusiastic voice. Once he engages again, slowly inch your hand down to his mouth on the toy. The pup should automatically release if he feels your skin near his mouth. If he does, praise and treat; if not, leave the room. He'll make the association that mouthing your skin results in you leaving the game. It will take a few tries, but he'll catch on and begin to quickly release and stop biting.

Help a puppy understand right from wrong! Bite inhibition will not be learned unless an owner teaches it to the puppy. Keep in mind that sensitive artist pups often learn after just one lesson. However, the party animal pup may need two or three rounds before catching on to the desired behavior.

THREE-STAGE PROCESS FOR BITE INHIBITION

1. **Create a gentle (soft) mouth.**

   Pups explore the world through their mouths and must be taught to control the pressure of a bite. It's up to owners to provide them with a message of "too hard" ("OUCH!").

2. **Teach a dog to release his hold on an object.**

   Incorporate the art of cooperative bargaining in the early stages of training. Offer a prized object in exchange for the one in his mouth. As he releases, mark "YES" and praise. This release technique is a building block for the DROP IT command featured in chapter 10.

3. **Teach DON'T BITE.**

   Have a zero-tolerance policy for biting and nipping human skin. When correcting and enforcing DON'T BITE, be sure to redirect behavior (tell him what to do) by providing bones and specific toys that are acceptable for biting and mouthing.

Note: When the correct items are being chewed, always reinforce with praise and petting. Establish that a soft, gentle mouth gets attention while a hard mouth causes you to leave. Educating a puppy about bite inhibition is important in the early stages of development. Start as soon as possible.

FINAL PUP NOTE

Never leave children unsupervised with puppies, or even older dogs. The sweetest dog in the world has the potential to bite. Kids may not realize that pulling a pup's tail or ears can hurt him and trigger a reaction. However, do include children in the training process. Owners with children who have achieved positive results by working on mouthing manners and bite inhibition techniques can advance to the UNDER TEN MOUTH-ING MANNERS: LICK ME LUV YOU technique as follows:

Apply a smear of cream cheese or peanut butter to your child's hand. This will allow the pup to enjoy a lick fest while understanding that skin, whether that of an adult or a child, is off limits to mouthing. Be sure to have your camera handy. This will be a keeper shot for the family album.

"CAN WE HAVE A PUPPY?"

"Helen and Henry had asked for a puppy for a while," said Allison. "They were at the right age and ready to be responsible for a puppy's needs." Getting a puppy is a big event in a household, especially one with children. The new family member will impact everyone and require adjustments to lifestyle. It's not realistic to expect kids under twelve to be capable of all the responsibilities that will be required.

My approach with children is to empower them to be educational team leaders for their puppy. It's about them feeling valued in the training process and being able to achieve results that manage a puppy's behavior. Involving children in the training benefits them in other areas of their lives as well. They learn that polite, self-assured leaders are capable of being firm with commands. Both ends of the leash become motivated while gaining trust and confidence in their relationship.

The Housekeeping of Housetraining

ousetraining ranks high on the list of why owners seek the professional services of a trainer. It's also a primary reason many dogs are relinquished to shelters. My proven system, if strictly followed, achieves success in housetraining in three to eight weeks. Puppies and rescue dogs may require additional time and supervision since they likely need to unlearn bad habits before acquiring appropriate ones. Adhering to a schedule with persistence and patience makes housetraining dogs of all ages possible.

Barring a serious medical condition, I've never met a dog that can't be housetrained. But I have met owners who neglected to make the necessary commitment to set their dogs up for success with potty training and other areas of housetraining. Housetraining requires dedicated, focused management, and it depends on the specifics related to the individual dog and his household and special circumstances.

Teaching a pooch to eliminate in a designated area isn't rocket science.

It's a taught command. Potty training, like all training, involves getting a dog to understand what you are asking of him. In the beginning he struggles to learn your language. However, this remarkable animal is capable of quickly adapting his behavior to his owner's requests.

RESCUE DOGS NEED POTTY TRAINING, TOO!

"Nan and I were at the opening of the Miami Film Festival," said Bruce. "When we came out of the theater, we noticed people crowding around the exit. It was stormy outside—rain, lightning and thunder. Police and all these people were standing there surrounding something. It was a dog tied to a metal storefront gate with an electric cord. She was well groomed and someone had elegantly tied a bow with the colors of France around her neck. The French, you know, really love dogs. Whoever had left her hoped someone would take pity on her and rescue her."

Billie Holiday succeeded in overcoming the down and dirty potty blues of housetraining.

American photographer and filmmaker Bruce Weber felt confident that he could secure a home for the black satin dog. "A girl was crying because her boyfriend wouldn't let her take the dog. There was also a guy who was upset. He said his building didn't allow dogs. After a police officer double-checked to be sure that no one in the crowd owned her, I decided to take her for the night."

Bruce recalled how the dog jumped into his van with all his friends and was not nervous but really well behaved.

Bruce had not planned to keep the four-month-old mixed breed with a glossy coat and ears that were quick to position into listening. On her chest is a surprising white patch that matches a rough-cut diamond and represents her bejeweled courage and tenacity. He named her Billie Holiday. Like the famed singer, she embraces a fierceness that ripples with sensitivity. Despite looking different from the other dogs in Weber's well-known and easy to recognize Golden Retriever pack, she's learned to fit in.

Some rescues have been severely punished for house-soiling mistakes. Instead of educating them, past owners might have struck them, left them tethered in backyards or isolated them somewhere in a home. Their housetraining has to start anew and proceed slowly and with patience. Training may take longer for rescues as they first need to rebuild trust with humans while establishing confidence that can only be created one step at a time. The bond with a new owner comes from developing a rewarding routine built on timely and precise corrections and re-directions.

The time frame for housetraining varies for each pup and rescue. Adhering to a strict and consistent schedule speeds up housetraining. Three to eight weeks is the general guideline for becoming proficient with elimination etiquette.

WHICH WAY TO THE LOO?

Weber's dogs cohabitate with him in Miami, the Hamptons and Manhattan. In Miami and the Hamptons, comprehending bathroom etiquette for Billie was simple. Scent markings left by the other dogs clued her in to understanding the appropriate elimination spots. However, the Big Apple turned out to be a big problem. Billie Holiday was a lady singing the down and dirty potty blues in the town known for its 24/7 intensity.

The backyard designated areas that Billie had come to identify with in Miami and the Hamptons were absent. She was introduced to a spacious Tribeca multilevel loft where she spent days on the fifth floor and evenings on the sixth. On her way outdoors, she had to enter a manually operated freight elevator with a huge metal gate that needed to be pulled up to open and down to close. Then she had yet another bladder-holding hurdle to manage as she made her way through a small foyer before she reached the front door and hit the pavement. Billie was also unaccustomed to being on a leash and dealing with urban canine stressors like:

- Concrete sidewalks
- Sharing the walkway with people, strollers, skateboarders and other dogs not belonging to her pack
- Fast-moving, unpredictable traffic and the sounds that come with it

As headquarters for Weber and his staff, the loft itself presented another set of challenging circumstances, such as:

- People constantly coming and going
- Phones, faxes, computers, printers, cameras and lights all ringing, clicking and flashing

The learned habits gained in Miami and the Hamptons were no longer useful. Everything here was new and unfamiliar. Billie couldn't rely on the retrievers for hints regarding the new toileting drill. They, too, were having their own issues with transitioning to the city and studio environment. There was no time to waste with Billie's training. It would include setting up a containment area for her and a strict adherence to a schedule for her food and water. Increased outings provided with "GO HERE" commands were done in areas likely marked by other dogs. Crating would also be implemented to help with Billie's training. Bruce, new to crate training, expressed concern about this technique, though he trusted me as a trainer.

A PLACE OF HER OWN

Owners resistant to crating their dogs overlook its value as more than just an effective and safe way to control and prevent elimination accidents. Billie was under a great deal of stress. Crating would simplify her housetraining confusion and establish boundaries. She'd have no battles to fight inside her den. A welcome rest, in a place of her own, would reduce her anxiety. Billie could then look at the world around her from a place of security, not fear. The hustle and bustle of the studio, the other dogs and everything else that was unfamiliar to Billie could be taken in from a place of calmness, not reactivity. The crate would give Billie structure, privacy and a way to acclimate herself to Bruce's life.

> A stressed dog can regress to peeing and pooping anywhere and everywhere.

HOUSETRAINING MATTERS

Dogs don't enter our lives knowing house rules or owners' expectations. Avoid approaching housetraining as "housebreaking." Instead, view it with a mind-set of fixing, not breaking, a behavior. Housetraining is about organizing and putting in place structure and an easy-to-follow routine. It involves choosing a desired elimination spot and not expecting a puppy to figure it out for himself. Without instruction or coaching, expect that he'll interpret "wherever" and "whenever" as permissible toileting. Clear communication is what shapes and strengthens the bond and puts housetraining in order. The idea is to prevent bad habits from forming.

Housetraining basics need to be decided by owners and should include:

- Deciding where you want your dog to eliminate: indoors (wee-wee pads), outdoors (backyard or curbside) or trained for both indoors and outdoors because of lifestyle needs.
- Setting up a containment area and being prepared to crate-train.
- Charting a schedule of feeding (meals and treats), walking, playtime, socializing and elimination.

The following list of seven must-ask questions serves as a checklist for canine housetraining. Housetraining is easier when you follow these user-friendly steps to get the job done with efficiency.

SEVEN MUST-ASK
HOUSETRAINING QUESTIONS

1. Has your dog had a veterinary health check to rule out any underlying medical condition such as bladder or urinary tract infection?

   Billie Holiday: *"Bruce knows the drill: Health checks rule out any underlying medical condition(s) that may be altering a dog's daily activities or behavior. I came back from the vet's with a clean bill of health."*

2. Is your dog in a contained space, or does he have free access to roam everywhere in your home?

   Billie Holiday: *"Well, let's just say Kate and Bruce at times agreed to disagree. Bruce was for unlimited access and Kate, less of a free spirit with regard to housetraining, said, 'Containment, log it and time it.'"*

3. Is food and water readily available for your dog at all times?

   Billie Holiday: *"Water needed to be available at all times for my five roommates. Crating kept me out of trouble and gave me downtime."*

4. Have there been any dietary changes?

   Billie Holiday: *"Yes, extra treats were given to me by staff, models and delivery people. This was part of my training program to counter my growling when strangers coming over to me overwhelmed me. Growling meant: 'Back off. If you want to say "hi" then make a proper introduction.' Kate understood this and came up with a plan—'Toss a treat and get a Billie greet.'*

   "It's important to note that I was behind in my socialization skills when I came into Bruce's life. Life in the Big Apple was about adjusting and adapting to everything around me. I was starting a new job, fitting into a new family and discovering that the backyard had been

redefined with concrete walkways, unnerving traffic and attitude . . . lots of urban attitude.

"FYI: Treats make you thirsty. For the purpose of housetraining, Kate made sure everyone logged down whenever I had water and peed outside. What goes in will come out."

5. How about stress? (e.g., a new baby, a home renovation, changes in the family dynamic)

    Billie Holiday: *"An intern, playing amateur trainer, claims he was told that by pinching my tail I would sit. Before I could slink away he pinched my tail! He scared the !!!** out of me. I peed everywhere. He claimed another trainer used the pinch technique to teach SIT. Really? Every time I saw that guy I peed and ran. That set my training back. Pretty sure that intern will not be putting dog 'trainer' on his résumé."*

6. Does elimination occur at certain times? (e.g., while you're at work, when you come home)

    Billie Holiday: *"'Whenever and wherever' was my motto. Kate had a different take: 'Here, not there.'"*

7. How many walks a day is your dog getting?

    Billie Holiday: *"In Miami we have easy access to the outdoors. The city has its attractions, but it does cramp my romp-and-roam style. Gotta love Bruce's groovy thinking, 'My dogs get six walks a day.'"*

THE MOTIVATORS AND THE PLACES TO GO

Peeing is self-rewarding for a dog. There was an urge, he peed or pooped and he's satisfied. The key to housetraining is making it rewarding for a dog to do it on cue in the appropriate place. Start with knowing where you want him to go to the bathroom.

"GOTTA GO" MOTIVATORS:

- Waking from a nap
- After play and activity
- After eating
- After drinking

WATCH FOR TELLTALE SIGNS OF ELIMINATION:
Sniffing, circling, squatting, whining and other behavior like spinning!!! Some will even shoot owners a *"GOTTA GO"* expression!!!

Relief Zones

- Indoors—on a wee-wee pad
- Outdoors—backyard
- Indoors and outdoors—pads and backyard
- Curbside—urban and suburban style
- Balcony/Porch—rural, suburban and urban

PEE HERE!

When you arrive home with a new puppy, immediately take him to the desired elimination spot. Don't allow him to race around and investigate the house. Take care of the first order of business: peeing and pooping. Next let him get settled into his containment area.

Rescue dogs may be older, but they also need to head straight to the designated loo. If you've been told that a dog has been housetrained, keep in mind that dogs don't generalize very well. He may have understood where to eliminate at the shelter or at another home but this is a new place for him. When you visit somewhere for the first time, I'm sure you've had to inquire, "Where's the bathroom?"

CUE WORDS FOR TOILETING

Dogs can be taught to toilet on command. The exact words used for the toileting command must always be the same. No exceptions. As a puppy prepares to relive herself, say with self-assured authority (think of yourself as the CEO, i.e., Canine Executive Officer), "Do your business," or "Go wee." The idea is to establish a phrase that's comfortable for you to say and be overheard by passersby. The real goal is having the pup associate the verbal cue with the elimination activity.

Rewarding Elimination

1. Bring treats when you lead your puppy to the designated elimination spot.
2. Avoid fanfare and don't create distractions. Remain silent and stand still. The goal is for her to relieve herself, not go for a walk.
3. Wait until she finishes, then praise "Good pee" or "Good poop" and give her a treat.

HALLELUJAH AND OTHER HOOPLA

When your dog finishes up on the paper or the curb, throw a celebratory poop party. Lavish on the praise and hand over a treat. Make it a "GOOD BOY" congratulatory event that can't be ignored. The truth is that this is a happy moment for both ends of the leash. Scooping the poop is checking off an item on an owner's to-do list.

If the pup's elimination is reliable and he's not a confused chewer (meaning the pup knows what is and is not appropriate to chew on), then expand his freedom in your home, one room at a time. For hands-free monitoring (umbilical cord training), fasten a six-foot leash to your belt loop or onto a sturdy table or chair leg. Your pooch will now have space outside the containment area and yet still be under your watchful eye.

OOPS!

Despite all the precautions, accidents will happen. Scolding a puppy that has had an accident will guarantee a setback in the process. Puppies live in the moment. They will not associate their mess made two hours, or even two minutes ago with your displeasure. Scientific studies reveal that rubbing a dog's nose in excrement or swatting him with rolled newspaper teaches the pup to be fearful of an owner, not where to pee or poop. In these situations, dogs may decide to defecate in remote areas of the home, such as in closets or the garage, to avoid being punished.

I've found spraying Grannick's Bitter Apple on previous elimination areas deters a dog from going back to that spot. Owners with sensitive noses will find that a few drops of peppermint oil, citrus oil or rosemary diluted in water and sprinkled around areas of the house may not housetrain a dog, but can provide the benefits of aromatherapy.

Four Easy Cleanup Steps

1. Blot as much as possible with a paper towel. Absorb as much as possible without pushing the urine deeper into the surface or allowing it to spread.

2. Saturate the area generously with Nature's Miracle, a pet-specific biological cleaner for house soiling mistakes. Let it soak in for five to ten minutes. Carpets or more heavily soiled areas may need more time (two to three hours) depending on the size of the spot.

3. You may need to repeat step 2. If it's carpeting, wait until the spot dries completely before reapplying Nature's Miracle.

4. Next use a product designed to clean carpet or hardwood floors. Nature's Miracle works great so you may not always need step 4.

Note: If you suspect a secret or discreet pee-er, consider purchasing an ultraviolet handheld flashlight to detect stains. The tiniest odor left behind will indicate to a pup that it's okay to relieve there. Remove all "PEE HERE" signage.

Possible Causes for Lapses in Housetraining

* Bladder infection
* Illness
* Digestive problems caused by food or food allergy
* Incontinence of older dog
* Lack of acclimation to being home alone
* Change of household environment (new baby, new apartment, construction next door)
* Lack of sufficient potty breaks
* Fear or separation anxiety

In the event you catch a dog mid-accident, make loud interruptive sounds, such as clapping or "EH-EH." Then pick up your pup and take him to the designated toilet area. When he finishes, praise him and give him a treat. During his race to pee, remain calm. Avoid overreacting in ways that could make a negative impression on him. The best approach is one that encourages your pup to realize: *"Not there but here. I go here and get relief and reward. Best to go here next time."* When accidents happen, it's preferable to clean them up without your pup watching you. This avoids him thinking it's an interactive game.

BLADDER SIZE

In the early stages of housetraining, a young puppy requires eight to ten trips during the day to relieve himself. His developing bladder will take three to six months to mature. At this stage, he's a baby requiring lots of toileting excursions and monitoring. Rescue and adopted dogs will need fewer bathroom outings than a puppy for the first two weeks, depending on medical and behavioral history.

How Often Do Puppies Need to Go?

Age	Bladder Capacity
6–8 weeks	30–45 minutes
12 weeks	90 minutes
18 weeks	2.5–3 hours

FIRST ORDER OF BUSINESS

Ready, set, go! Start with a patient and attentive routine. Keep in mind that there's a great deal being asked of a puppy, rescue or even an adult dog entering an unfamiliar household. The job can be done in a reasonable amount of time if you follow the 4 C's: containment area (p. 90), crate training, consistency and calm energy.

If you are an owner at your wits' end, start by putting together the containment area discussed in the previous chapter—a specially designated spot in your home for the puppy. The space becomes his schoolyard, playground, toilet (for short-term or long-term use), mess hall, bedroom and calm zone.

CRATE TRAINING 101

I endorse crate training because it works as a positive reinforcement management tool. When used as recommended, it goes beyond housetraining fundamentals. Crating provides a dog with a safe and acceptable way to travel on planes. If recovering from an injury, a crate will limit a dog's movements. It can also serve as a transportable evacuation device during an emergency. Crating removes confusion in housetraining by providing stability, sanctuary and security for the new family member. It serves as a safe haven while he gets acquainted with and acclimated to boundaries and house rules.

Owners gain leadership status by complying with a crating routine that adheres to a strict and well-timed schedule. A dog gains trust in the crate once it's associated with a place where good things happen. Owners and dogs build reliance on and trust of one another. This develops and conditions canine responsiveness to the GO IN YOUR CRATE command because dogs find it rewarding behavior to do so.

Proper timing is the biggest hurdle to overcome. Strict scheduling reinforced by patience and consistency can't be overstated to owners. Crate training teaches a dog what is being expected of him in housetraining. It doesn't reprimand a dog. Instead, it provides the instinctual incentive to not want to eliminate where he sleeps because it goes against his nature to soil in his den (crate).

The dog that still has an occasional accident is not fully housetrained. Consider retooling his training using the techniques in this chapter. Letting unwanted behavior and bad habits persist is problematic. It makes housetraining more difficult and it takes longer to resolve.

Soiling mistakes shouldn't be blamed on a dog. It's the owner's responsibility to teach a dog where and when to eliminate. Crating provides a safe management tool for owners to prevent bad habits from forming. The right combination of management and training accomplishes successful housetraining.

Crating Benefits	Functions and Purposes
Security	Appeals to a dog's instinctual desire for a den-like structure.
Self-confidence	Sets a puppy up for success by reducing pee and poop accidents.
Self-reliance	Prepares a pup for handling alone time.
Privacy	Serves as a time-out device for pups and owners needing breaks.
Behavioral Health	Discourages and reduces separation anxiety in many cases.
Practicality	Gets pups used to confinement that may be required at the vet's, the groomer's and during car trips or on airplanes.
Transport Device	Contains a pup if he is injured and his mobility must be limited.

FEATURED TRAINING TECHNIQUE: CRATE TRAINING

Quick Description: Crate Training

It conditions a dog to accept being in a crate.

A timed routine teaches a pup to control his bladder—a win for the owner. With a safe space to relax and sleep, a pup has his own residence—a win for the pup.

"Good things happen inside here" should be what a dog feels.

Note: A crate should never be used for punishment or as a bathroom facility. The dog must have only a positive association with his crate. Everything he wants and needs—toys, bones, praise, meals and water—should be available there.

Fit: The puppy should be able to stand up comfortably without crouching and be able to turn around inside the crate. A minimum of two inches of space should be available between the pup and the crate on all sides. Too much space may entice him to have an accident. If you purchase a crate that will accommodate a puppy as he grows, be sure to insert partition dividers.

Items Inside Crate: a light blanket (the familiar scent will provide comfort), a toy (not stuffed) and a yummy chew bone.

Goals:

- Prevent potty accidents
- Teach alone time
- Ensure proper amount of sleep
- Provide a safe haven in homes, especially those with children or lots of activity

Benefits: Owners who crate train gain greater flexibility in managing their dogs' behaviors. Crating for traveling and emergencies makes life easier for both ends of the leash.

Crate Style Recommendation: If a pup is a destructive chewer, use a wire crate or airline cargo carrier, not one made of wood. I prefer classic wire crates that are durable, easy to fold and well ventilated.

CRATES—CLASSIC TO PENTHOUSE:

1. SHERPA   2. WIRE CRATE

3. CUSTOMIZED CRATE   4. AIRLINE CARRIER

Crate Training Steps

1. Location matters so avoid high-traffic entryways. A kitchen, bathroom, bedroom or at the side of a living room works.

2. Secure the crate door open during the introduction phase. Avoid closing it suddenly and startling the puppy. For a wire crate, place a lightweight fabric over the top to enhance the den-like atmosphere.

3. Toss high-value treats into the crate, or even outside the crate door. Command "GO IN YOUR CRATE" (GO FIND IT) while doing this.

4. With an excited tone, praise the pup every time he moves toward the crate. (JOLLY EFFECT, p. 21)

5. Continue tossing treats into the crate. Turn it into a fun game. The pup will begin to understand that every time he runs into the crate, something good happens with treats and his owner's enthusiastic energy. The IN YOUR CRATE GAME/GO FIND IT CRATE GAME should continue for ten repetitions.

6. If the pup's behavior has become reliable and he's accustomed to running into the crate, advance to placing a yummy filled Kong, Busy Buddy dispenser chew toy, bone or bully stick into the crate. The goal is to get him to adjust to longer periods of time inside the crate.

7. Attempt to close the door once he's comfortable and busy chewing his treat, but don't latch it.

8. If the dog is uncomfortable with the crate door closed, smear peanut butter or cream cheese on the inside of the door, then latch it closed. The puppy may continue chewing his bone or start licking the crate door. Wait until he's done with one of those activities, then calmly let him out without any attention. Reserve your "JOLLY" attention for whenever he approaches, not exits, the crate.

9. Repeat steps 3–8 up to five times a day in ten-minute increments. Feeding times can be optimal crating opportunities with positive reinforcement benefits.

Start with one minute, then two to three, five and then ten. You can sit near the crate at first, then slowly inch your way away. If your pooch has a hard time with you inching away, throw treats into the crate every time you move away so he develops a positive association with your leaving. Pup: *"Good things happen when my owner moves away."* Ten-minute increments inside the crate are recommended to ensure the puppy is comfortable with the crate and has a positive association with it. Successful dog training is built on repetition and consistency. The more you do it, the faster the dog will learn.

Crate Do's	Crate Don'ts
DO praise and act excited every time the puppy approaches the crate.	DON'T push a pup past his toileting limits. You don't want him to urinate or poop in his crate. That would create a negative association with the crate.
DO turn the crate into a dispenser for everything the dog wants. Schedule his feedings and water breaks in the crate (remove bowls when finished). Place toys, bones and chew toys inside. Let it become a desired destination for him.	DON'T use the crate as punishment.
DO go at the pup's pace when introducing him to the crate. Slow and steady will win his confidence and trust.	DON'T force a pup into a crate. Review the crate-training steps featured in this chapter. They focus on desensitizing a pup to a crate.
DO be sure to leave him with a safe chew bone. It gives him something to do.	DON'T leave food and water in the crate. The idea is to control a pup's food and water intake while teaching bladder control and determining an elimination schedule.

Crate Do's	Crate Don'ts
DO cover the sides for fewer distractions. That will encourage him to use his den for a restful crash pad for naps and nighttime.	DON'T go to a pup when he whines in the crate. It reinforces unwanted behavior. Instead, wait two or three seconds for him to settle down (capture a moment of silence), then go to him.

> Puppies secrete ADH, an antidiuretic hormone, which allows them to hold their bladders overnight.

THREE COMMON HOUSTRAINING QUESTIONS

Question: I want my puppy to learn to go outdoors, but he isn't fully vaccinated. Do you have a suggestion?

Response: Take a wee-wee pad outdoors and follow the Rewarding Eliminations steps outlined earlier in the chapter: (1) Pick spot. (2) Avoid distractions. (3) Wait until he finishes, then praise "Good pee" or "Good poop" and give him a treat. The pad keeps the pup from eliminating in an unsafe area, reducing the health threat if he's not fully vaccinated.

Question: My puppy won't go on the pad. She'll sit on it but then walk away and pee on the floor. What am I doing wrong?

Response: Create the pee incentive! Next time she pees or poops, take a fresh pad and dab a little of the elimination on it. The scent will encourage your pup to make the association: pad = elimination spot.

Question: How do you switch from wee-wee pads to outdoor eliminations?

Response: The pad-to-pavement phase is about incrementally cutting
down the size of the pad. In short time, a curb, grass or sidewalk will
become the elimination surface.

PSYCHE PEE WALK

Is there a special knack to housetraining? Well, for those owners with a
puppy that waits until he gets back inside to pee, maybe just a bit. Take
the little guy out and expect him to pull his "Thanks for the walk" routine: *"Now that I'm inside, I gotta go."* However, this time instead of
opening the door to go back inside, head right back out to the street.
Don't walk, but for five to ten minutes, just stand in an area where it's appropriate to eliminate. You may need to repeat this psyche-out routine for
five to ten repetitions. That gives the owner two advantages: first, a developing bladder that'll give in, and second, the "no pleasure stroll" until his
business is done. This reinforces desired behavior. The pup will figure it
out faster than you think. Keep in mind that no matter what he's telling
you, he's the puppy and you're the trainer, not the reverse.

NEW BEGINNINGS

Working with Bruce's dog Billie Holiday brought back old boarding
school memories. Back then when I was the new kid in class I lacked the
confidence to raise my hand when teachers asked questions. I was shy and
felt awkward. I knew the answers, but I was unable to say them out loud.
It was hard for me to express myself because I was afraid I didn't fit in
and I was different from the other kids.

Some of Billie's challenges paralleled mine. I recognized them and knew how to resolve them. Billie needed encouragement. Golden retrievers populated her boarding school. They were more familiar with the dynamic household routine and secure in the bond with their owners. Billie neither looked like them nor shared their genetic traits. Trying to figure out how to fit in and to familiarize and adapt to the active and revolving urban and rural lifestyle left Billie overwhelmed, confused and fearful. I knew she simply needed to build up her confidence, trust in others and become responsive in her behavior. Setting Billie Holiday up for success became personal for me. I equated her unique canine instincts with my experience of being the new kid on the block.

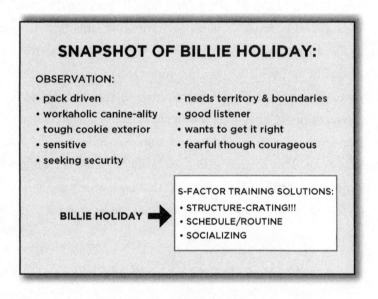

SNAPSHOT OF BILLIE HOLIDAY:

OBSERVATION:

- pack driven
- workaholic canine-ality
- tough cookie exterior
- sensitive
- seeking security
- needs territory & boundaries
- good listener
- wants to get it right
- fearful though courageous

BILLIE HOLIDAY ➡

S-FACTOR TRAINING SOLUTIONS:
- STRUCTURE-CRATING!!!
- SCHEDULE/ROUTINE
- SOCIALIZING

STRUCTURE, SCHEDULING AND SOCIALIZING

In order to change canine behavior, a strong commitment from the owners and the pet's inner circle is required. Bruce and Nan were exceptional owners. They embraced the training process and made sure their staff was on board. Structure, scheduling and socializing were patiently integrated into housetraining.

Structure

I placed a crate next to Bruce's desk and covered it with fabric to cut down the stimulus of the other dogs and minimize other loft distractions. Bruce was visible to Billie and, when he wasn't there, his scent gave her reassurance and comfort. The all-in-one function of the crate provided structure, reduced stress and enabled her to manage and control her bladder.

Once inside the crate, Billie was able to calmly acclimate to the loft, people, dogs and other dynamics from a safe haven. The secure space allowed her to drop her guard and get some needed rest. People sometimes overlook that sleep reduces stress. A Kong filled with treats or a chew bone was always left in her crate to occupy her time when she was awake.

Crate Training Techniques Specific to Billie Holiday

1. Billie's reserved personality craved a defined space. Lisa Merkle, Weber's studio manager, informed me that, when Bruce was out shooting, Billie would scoot into the cubbyhole area of her desk. It was her way of creating a makeshift crate.
2. Lots of "IN YOUR CRATE" and "GO FIND IT" games familiarized her with the crate. At the same time, they desensitized her to it. All meals were served inside the crate. Treats and food provided incentives and rewards. A positive association was established.
3. Billie loved having the opportunity to tune out other aspects of her surroundings. The energy from others let her know she was doing things right, and this helped to build her confidence.
4. The studio's comings and goings, which once overwhelmed Billie,

were used to our training advantage. Billie no longer needed to jockey for territory, but she still didn't want to be alone. Crating gave her a residence while the hustling and bustling people and dogs became her beloved "pack," making her assimilation to the crate much easier.

Scheduling

Like anyone new to a city, Billie needed a routine. She was taken out to pee and poop six times a day. Once she did her business, she could be out of the crate for thirty minutes with supervision. A schedule determines a dog's bathroom habits and makes the use of a chart advisable. It should include the activity times and notes for:

- Waking
- Feeding
- Water
- Crating
- Play and exercise
- Pees and poops

This rigid schedule establishes good canine habits, reliability and results. Billie's story exemplifies what can be achieved when implementing and adhering to sensible guidelines. Structure (crate) and schedule gave her the opportunity to discover the dog she was always meant to be.

Socializing

My clients often hear me say, "Exercise, exercise, exercise and socialize." No housetraining is complete without proper socialization. Rescue dogs often enter their new homes suffering from trauma, a lack of confidence or other issues. Billie Holiday was no exception. Her situation was even trickier since it involved multiple locations, new owners, a revolving door of staff, models and service personnel and five other dogs.

Steps for Billie Holiday's Debutante Ball

1. For the social setup, everyone in the room was prepared to toss a treat to Billie as they walked by her. This was cooperation training at work. Now people were rewarding her and she began to see them as welcoming, not threatening. This Debutante Ball game helped her accept having lots of people around her.

2. On the second round of her gala, we moved closer to the individuals. They touched her and gave her treats. Everyone was told to make slow movements and avoid jerking motions. The tone of their voices had to be in JOLLY EFFECT (p. 21) mode and they had to reach under, not over, her head. (Preferably under the muzzle in a neutral, calm and nonthreatening manner.)

3. When Billie was placed in her crate, the treats kept coming. Anyone passing by was encouraged to toss her a treat. The growling Ms. Holiday was changing her tune and she began to look forward to the attention as much as the treats.

MODEL BEHAVIOR

It was crucial to get Billie housetrained. Bruce and his staff were in the midst of shoots for *Vogue*, *Vanity Fair*, Abercrombie & Fitch and other well-known clients. Disruptions were becoming too frequent and were impacting the studio dynamics. "Kate taught me that consistency, structure and patience would pay off with housetraining Billie," said Bruce. "She was right."

Billie gained confidence and poise as she learned to hit her mark on the pavement and in my studio. Her model behavior captured Bruce's heart and his camera lens. "Anna Wintour [editor in chief of American *Vogue*] became a big fan of hers [Billie]. Every time I photograph for American *Vogue* and use Billie in a shot, she always ends up in a full page by herself. It's quite funny. I have all these beautiful golden retrievers and it's Billie who ends up in a full page for *Vogue*."

The combination of Bruce's willingness to do whatever was needed, his staff's complete cooperation and Billie Holiday's courage and determination made her housetraining a success. Bruce: "For the rest of my life, I'll always have a rescue dog because I think they teach you so much about what's really important. Housetraining may have been more challenging but the rewards have made me an even better owner."

Billie has learned that life is about adapting, coping and accepting help.

Tailgating

Tailgating is a dog's supervised introduction to people, things and sensory experiences. It prepares puppies and dogs for life—especially when it isn't always predictable. Think of it as the nursery school, preschool and lifelong education that cultivates desirable canine social manners and coping skills. It shapes a dog's temperament into reliable behavior.

Tailgating is what helps a pup assimilate and adjust to any and all potential challenges. Each time a pup is introduced to something new, we want an owner to assist and guide him to form positive lifelong associations with that situation, person or object. The development of canine coping skills is a primary building block for ensuring good behavior inside your home and elsewhere. It turns dogs into team players as they adapt to the family dynamics and the world around them with greater ease. Did I mention it's also fun?

Under-socialization, the opposite of tailgating, sets dogs up for failure in life. An example of this is the puppy that, prior to receiving his full vaccination, is given limited and restricted exposure to other dogs, people and experiences. He will be behind in his social development. The isolation will impact his ability to handle and adjust to life around him. This pup is likely to be reactive and not relaxed in new situations and encounters. These are the types of pups most often relinquished to shelters.

TAILGATING INTERVENTION

Dynamic and interactive tailgating skills (social schooling) helped Legs conquer his anxious and once-timid behavior.

"Can I make this work?" When he spoke those five words, New York University president John Sexton was expressing a combination of panic, frustration, confusion and doubt. "I took the notion of having my first dog, a Havenese, very seriously," he explains. "I strictly adhered to my veterinarian's advice to keep Legs isolated and kept indoors until fully vaccinated." Sexton, a do-it-yourself trainer, had also been applying "old drill-sergeant techniques" that further hampered and challenged Legs's tailgating socialization skills.

Canine Confessions of Do-It-Yourself Trainers

- "I tried rubbing his nose in his mess, but that didn't stop Legs from going all over the house."
- "Last night I came home from work and went around looking because I just knew Spaulding, my whippet, had done it somewhere. He looked guilty and ran away from me as I walked near him."
- "Whenever Bandit jumped on the couch, I swatted her in the behind with a rolled-up newspaper. Now when I call her, she won't come to me."
- "If I want Jazz to sit, I push her behind down. The other day when I did it, she nipped me."

Methods like the above punish unwanted behavior without redirecting it or getting to the root cause of it. The puppy isn't thinking about right or wrong behavior in that moment. He's responding to an owner's erratic behavior and saying, *"I don't like that!"* and *"You scare me."*

"I came dangerously close to putting Legs in a position where he would need years of therapy," said John. "When I explained to Kate what I'd been doing, she blanched and said, 'My heavens, you can't do that. You don't shout at a dog or punish a puppy. You've got to motivate a dog.' I realized in that moment that I was in a whole different world when it came to contemporary dog training. Thank God she saved me from the old-school materials I had accumulated."

OLD SCHOOL

Positive reinforcement training differs from the old-school approach in many ways. Using harsh punishment to teach a dog is one such old-school method. John was applying force and aversive corrections to curb unwanted behavior. The result was unsuccessful for both owner and pup. Legs, who was still so young, was becoming afraid of John and the other end of the leash was sensing that.

Cooperation training, using positive reinforcement techniques, in my opinion is leaps ahead of old-school methods, especially since it gets owners to realize that socialization is an absolute necessity to the upbringing of a well-behaved puppy.

IS YOUR DOG SOCIALIZED?

It was clear that Legs needed a tailgating intervention. The following typifies exchanges I have with owners who contact me about housetraining, but also need tailgating exposure:

KATE: Is your dog socialized?

OWNER: Absolutely. He gets along great with my other dog.

KATE: Does he get along with other dogs?

OWNER: Oh no. He doesn't like other dogs. In fact, he's not welcome at the local dog park.

KATE: How is he with children?

OWNER: We don't let him near children. He nipped my nephew.

KATE: When deliveries arrive, is he calm or reactive?

OWNER: The UPS man is terrified of him. Can you imagine being afraid of an eight-pound dog?

Summary: A dog with only one dog playmate is not socialized. If his interactions with other dogs, children and adults are reactive and aggressive, then the dog is *not* fully socialized.

As for the UPS man's fears about an eight-pound dog, all dogs, large and small, are capable of biting and exhibiting aggressive behavior. Tailgating is about eliminating unwanted reactivity by providing a dog with all the resources necessary to become an outstanding and well-received canine.

Progressive veterinarians and the American Veterinary Society of Animal Behavior (AVSAB) favor sensible and supervised early exposure to people, places, objects and other healthy dogs. So do I.

CLOCK IS TICKING

Six to sixteen weeks of age is the most impressionable phase and the optimal learning opportunity for a puppy. Isolating Legs during his optimal learning stage was done with the best of intentions. John was looking out for the health of his dog.

Legs could be housetrained, but he was way behind in his socialization skills. At four months old, he was displaying signs of canine stress, such as:

- Timid behavior
- Being easily spooked by people and noises
- Being hand shy
- Cringing and crouching body positions

- Backing away when someone came near him too fast
- Downward head and tail
- Darting eyes

During the puppy stage, backing away, hand shyness and other anxious traits may look adorable to onlookers and owners, but they can often be telltale signs of a potential canine clock ticking. As a dog's fear progresses over time, responsive reactions build up inside him. Without proper training, a puppy's behavior is likely to become aggressive and reactive. The displacement signs discussed in the first chapter should not be ignored. The subtleties of a canine yawn, nervous licking or sideways head turns—cut-off and calming signals—represent canine language. They must be mindfully decoded in order for an owner to best understand and raise a well-adjusted and balanced dog.

The three-month-old puppy that learns that a low guttural growl keeps others at bay might delight family members and amuse guests. But the same behavior at six to twelve months will no longer be entertaining or tolerated. The dog hasn't been given the right set of circumstances to succeed in life. No living creature chooses to live in fear. Fear is generated from perceived threats against one's survival.

TAILGATING INGREDIENTS

Tailgating brings all of the ingredients from the previous chapters together. These include:

- Understanding the four primal canine drives (pack, prey, flight and fight)
- Canine-ality types (academic and methodical thinker, sensitive artist, workaholic, party animal)

- Sherlock Canine Holmes (owner observational skills)
- Canine speak (reading canine body language)
- Owner assessment (the array of practical and lifestyle concerns that impact both ends of the leash)
- Puppyscaping (interior designing for the four-legged)
- Housetraining (taking care of potty business)

Commitment to tailgating starts with earning a dog's trust and with the first "LOOK-AT-ME" moment. The command really says to a dog, "You can rely on me. Turn to me for guidance and support. That's what I'm here for." It's a hands-free command that demonstrates inspired leadership, not dominance, over a dog. Overlooked in obedience training is its value in socializing a dog. Commands are active tailgating tools that allow owners to redirect a dog's behavior while establishing a close and cooperative bond.

LET'S GET THIS PARTY STARTED

When it comes to exposing a pup to anything and everything, owners don't have a moment to waste. An owner should invite lots of people, things and sensory experiences into a dog's tailgating life (review Seven Days of Discovery, p. 79). Expect that some folks will show up without RSVPing, or simply crash the party. Be prepared for a neighborhood off-leash dog, a Girl Scout knocking on the door selling cookies or an electric storm that brings wind, thunder and buckets of rain. Preparing a dog for life's unanticipated moments in a nurturing, supportive and supervised way will help him grow into a confident canine while preventing future behavioral problems.

A tailgating party teaches a pup to be calm and nonreactive to his surroundings. It's meant to familiarize him with various challenges and enable him to best analyze and understand that new people, objects, situations and circumstances are nonthreatening. Without owner-supervised exposure, canine triggers on the invite list can potentially elicit a fearful response from a puppy. A tailgating soiree helps prevent negative impressions from forming. It also reduces reactive behavior such as lunging, cowering and growling by redirecting and curbing a dog's impulse control with commands or other activities. The idea is to control the experiences a pup encounters by using training tools that I provide in the next section.

Tailgating Benefits

1. Improves a dog's coping skills and enables him to adjust to a variety of circumstances, especially an owner's lifestyle.
2. Builds canine esteem and confidence.
3. Provides mental and physical stimulation.
4. Improves obedience skills.

Tailgating sets a dog up for success in life by getting him to be relaxed and resilient around novel experiences while building his confidence.

Potential Tailgate Guests

A dog's reactivity has a great deal to do with his being unfamiliar with people, surfaces, objects, locations, sounds and activities. Anyone and everything can be a potential tailgate guest to your dog.

The following is a list of likely guests:

People

- In uniform
- Loud talkers
- Homeless
- Wearing boots
- Disabled
- Speaking with an accent
- Animated
- Laughing
- Silent types
- Wearing sunglasses

Surfaces

- Slippery
- Cold
- Wet
- Muddy
- Wood chips
- Pea gravel
- Mulch
- Dirt
- Cobblestones
- Granite

Objects

- Umbrella
- Vacuum cleaner
- Broom
- Garbage bin
- Shoe
- Hair dryer
- Shopping cart

- Suitcase
- Purse
- Walking cane

Locations

- Garage
- Barn
- Subway
- Outdoor café
- Street fair
- Dog park
- Parking lot
- Outskirts of a playground
- Pool area
- Patio

Sounds

- Speakerphone
- Fire alarm
- Television
- Fireworks
- Dishwasher
- Buzzer
- Crinkling plastic bags
- Online game noises (blasts, crashes and gunfire)
- Screaming kids
- Power tools

Activities

- In-flight traveling in Sherpa bag
- Car rides
- Tollbooths

- Strangers approaching
- Elevators
- Snowdrifts
- Curbing to eliminate
- Crowded streets
- Unleashed dogs
- Being cornered

Dining Experiences

- Plastic bowl
- Metal bowl
- Plate
- Kong or other treat dispenser
- On the stoop
- Multi-species household (cats and dogs)
- Park bench
- Airport
- Lap
- While training

TAILGATING TOOLS

Primary training techniques facilitate the tailgating experience:

Technique	Purpose
Exposure	Identify potential canine triggers.
	Introduce a dog to potential canine triggers in a calm, supervised manner.
	Instill canine confidence and balanced social skills.

Technique	Purpose
Desensitizing	Systematically get a dog accustomed to a sound, situation or object.
Habituation	A dog adapts over time and gets used to a stimulus or trigger.
	Early touching and handling of a puppy is recommended and gets him used to grooming as well as to veterinarian exams.

Exposure

Exposure means introducing a dog to a multitude of unfamiliar objects, elements, situations, people and other dogs—at the earliest stage of his life. Exposure to neutral, unpleasant, even pleasant sounds, motions, smells and visuals is undertaken with the express purpose of curbing canine behavioral problems. Calmly integrating exposures into a dog's life establishes nonthreatening associations with potential canine triggers and stimuli.

Desensitization

The process of desensitization involves incremental exposure to a potential canine trigger such as a street sweeper or vacuum cleaner. A pup needs to become familiar with and accustomed to new things in stages:

1. Start with introductions at a distance the pup can handle. Allow the pup to see the object or canine trigger. If he's calm or inquisitive, be quick to reward that behavior with a treat and praise.
2. Decrease the distance and continue to reward his nonreactive behavior with praise and treats.

3. If he's curious, let him get closer to the object or canine trigger.

4. Don't overdo the exposure.

5. The goal of desensitization is to take successful incremental steps and not risk overload.

6. Owners' actions need to be immediate in these situations to mark them properly as absolute and firm associations. The dog's mindset should be:

Fido: *"I see the vacuum or street sweeper, but no worries, as these both bring me treats. Pay attention to the reward, not the distraction."*

Habituation

Dogs that are properly exposed to certain things, such as crowd noise or being in an elevator for a long period of time, will gradually adapt and become less reactive. That's because they've become habituated to the stimulus, condition or situation. If you ever lived next to a train station or busy highway, the noise may initially have been unnerving, but over time you learned to tune it out. Dogs have that same ability and consequently can adapt to loud, crowded and noisy places and conditions.

A change in the amount of exposure to a tailgating guest can impact a dog's reactivity. An owner with a born and bred city dog may find relocating to a rural setting an unnerving experience for his dog. Tailgating "guests" such as lawn mowers, cows and peace and quiet need to become familiar to the pup and incorporated into his environment. The same owner, moving back to the city a year or so later, might find his dog unnerved by the urban environment, despite having once lived in that habitat. That's because the dog is no longer habituated to the sound of sirens, crowded elevators and street sweepers. He'll need to be reacquainted (exposed) with sights, sounds, tastes, touches and smells associated with city living.

PUTTING THE PARTY TOGETHER

Tailgating tools are behavior modification techniques used to stabilize and develop greater reliability of a dog's temperament and behavior. The idea is to use them to modify, shape and reinforce his behavior to fit comfortably into your lifestyle and household. I urge owners to be innovative with their tailgating guest list. Think out of the box and replicate circumstances that may be challenging for a dog. Anything that stimulates the five senses of a dog (sight, sound, taste, touch and smell) is a welcome guest. We want to prepare and condition a dog to deal with whatever arises in life with a "no big deal" attitude.

Tailgating is what allows the owner to best understand and determine the number of interactions (exposures) a dog needs to become familiar with (desensitized to), adjusted to and relaxed around (habituated to) a particular party guest. Below is a Tailgating Interaction Chart with seven categories of tailgating guests: people, surfaces, objects, locations, sounds, activities and dining experiences.

Tailgating Interaction Chart

Interaction	Monday	Tuesday	Wednesday	Thursday	Friday	Saturday	Sunday
Person wearing a hat	2x			5x		1x	
Concrete surface	3x		1x		2x		1x
Drugstore (pet-friendly)	1x			1x			

Hair dryer	1x	1x	1x	1x	1x	1x	1x
Playground			1x			2x	2x

The number of interactions that lower reactivity and develop reliable behavior will vary. There are also many other factors, such as:

- Consistency of exposure, desensitization and habituation
- Owner's abilities, lifestyle and schedule
- Canine-ality and genetics of a dog

Successful tailgating parties are insurance policies that reduce the likely occurrences of a dog:

- Biting a child or others
- Becoming aggressive with another dog
- Shutting down and becoming a ticking time bomb

There's nothing cookie-cutter about the tailgating process. It's a personalized training technique. The Tailgating Interaction Chart serves as a guide for creating the perfect tailgating party. Socializing can happen from day one without concern about full vaccination. Visitors can arrive wearing hats, sunglasses or boots. They can talk in soft or loud voices.

Another health-safeguarding option for puppy tailgating parties is a short car ride around the neighborhood. From a distance the pup will see other dogs of various breeds and sizes and observe many other tailgating guests. This will advance his training and make him amenable to accepting change, new people, challenges and interactions with greater ease.

Playing with your dog is tailgating. So is holding him in your lap. The sooner the tailgating begins, the less unwanted behavior a dog has to unlearn.

PIVOTAL TAILGATING STEPS FOR LEGS

Legs was on the verge of becoming a social recluse. He needed to get out and about before his timid, cowering behavior developed into a bigger problem. John understood that the traditional methods he was using on Legs had evoked fear, not trust. In my first session with John he turned to Legs and said, "Oh, I'm so sorry, Legs." He then turned to me and asked, "Can I fulfill my responsibilities to Legs in a way that is both deserved and needed?"

Taking care of a dog means more than just feeding (diet), exercising and housetraining. Raising a healthy, happy and vibrant pooch is also about providing nurturing care for his emotional well-being. He needs to be fully engaged with his indoor and outdoor environments. At sixteen weeks of age, Legs had been limited to an overly generous containment area. Considering the circumstances, my reply to John's question was to give the training process a month, and then reevaluate the situation.

Legs lives near Washington Square Park, a place full of people, kids, musicians, skateboarders, joggers and all sorts of characters, sights and sounds. He was terrified of it all. The first time I reached for Legs he was shaking, scared and nervous. He cowered, and when I took him outdoors he shut down.

An intensive desensitization program began with all of Legs's feeding taking place outdoors. Food is rewarding to dogs and acts as a distraction to frightening stimuli. The food supplies the incentive.

Tailgating Steps for Legs

- Legs needed incentive to leave his home. He was working off his flight drive, which stemmed from being under-socialized. Gaining his trust needed to happen first and that would come from supplying him with high-value food outdoors. For two weeks he was only fed in the park, during walks and anywhere else that took him out of his comfort zone. He started to understand that going outside was rewarding for him. It's like any of us going to work so we can get paid.
- His pack drive that attached him to John was high. He needed to learn to be accepting of others. That was resolved by transferring the feedings and walks to other people, including doormen, kids, a uniformed individual, someone in a wheelchair and students. It's important to rear a dog that can adapt to others. Velcro dogs can regress and become separation anxiety cases. Tailgating pushes a dog toward greater independence and a balanced temperament.
- Working the LOOK-AT-ME command helped Legs gain coping skills. The command was especially helpful around challenging tailgate guests, such as thunder, sirens and street sweepers.
- Legs was enrolled in puppy class where a sound-effects CD was used to introduce and acclimate him to sounds of thunder, fireworks, jackhammering and other noises.
- A rotation of different dog walkers were put into service to help Legs adjust to new people, and dog day care was implemented to expand dog-on-dog interactions.

Training Techniques Specific to Legs

The following outlines the specific techniques applied for John and Legs:

Session	Training Techniques
1–3	Implemented tailgating
	Restaged containment area
	Puppy-proofed household
	Set up schedule and elimination chart
	Emphasized a consistent routine
	Instructed and engaged the following commands: LOOK-AT-ME, TOUCH TARGET and SHORT & SWEET MEET & GREET
4	Command: SIT and DOWN
5	Command: STAY
6	Command: WALKING ON LEASH
7	Command: LEAVE IT
8	Command: COME
9–10	Innovative training sessions provided incentive for both ends of the leash. Legs had a natural talent to FETCH on cue. John's final exam included advancing the FETCH command to include GO GET IT, BRING IT and DROP IT.
	Legs loves to perform and John loves baseball so this created a tailored, lifestyle-specific, win-win training dynamic that went like this:
	GO GET IT (turns Legs into an outfielder)
	BRING IT (Legs as shortstop)

> DROP IT (catcher who also can learn to put away his balls and toys).
>
> Good teachers make learning fun.

FEATURED TRAINING TECHNIQUE: SHORT & SWEET MEET & GREET

Quick Description: Dog-to-Dog SHORT & SWEET MEET & GREET

Establish a goal of meeting as many friendly dogs as possible. Be mindful that, in a city, dogs need to be on-leash. Meeting five or more dogs per walk is a good practice.

Goal: to help encourage a dog's social skills and teach good manners with canine greetings. Dogs isolated from other dogs can lunge or become threatened by canine encounters. Resolve that reactive behavior early with SHORT & SWEET MEET & GREETs.

Dog-to-Dog SHORT & SWEET MEET & GREET Steps

1. Start by teaching your pooch to LOOK-AT-ME (p. 28) or SIT (p. 56) and STAY (p. 174) before exiting your front door. The idea is to keep a dog's impulse control in check before going outside. Think of this step as a dress rehearsal.
2. Search for friendly-looking dogs and people who are not distracted—

SHORT & SWEET MEET & GREETS are canine good manners.

ideally both owners and dogs exhibit good energy and have relaxed attitudes.

3. Once a good match is spotted, be sure to ask, "Is your dog friendly?" I suggest doing this when you are six to ten feet away to avoid a reactive dog or owner. A tip that works is offering the universal thumbs-up gesture along with a smile and adding, "Is your dog friendly?" Or "Does your dog like other dogs?"

4. If you get an OK sign then quickly ask your pooch to LOOK-AT-ME, and command SIT. Then release the command before giving another: "GO SAY HI." Offer encouragement by swiftly moving your pooch toward the other dog. Don't drag him to a MEET & GREET.

5. If the other person replies, "Sometimes," or "Not really," accept the owner's word and move on. A confident canine mind-set needs to be established before the dog can comprehend an unfriendly encounter: "Yikes, that little guy is having a bad day. Oh well, I know

not all dogs are grouchy! Let's go find someone else to talk to." Healthy rebound skills will develop over time, but first put in place a foundation of canine confidence.

6. Once the dogs are nose to nose, keep a loose leash and let them sniff each other. Praise your dog while they are sniffing and investigating each other.

7. For the city dwellers facing many dogs at once, keep this dog-to-dog SHORT & SWEET MEET & GREET activity limited to twenty to thirty seconds, then move on. This is a preventative measure that avoids leash tangles and greetings ending on a bad note. Be sure to refocus your dog to LOOK-AT-ME before leaving and searching out another tailgating party opportunity.

8. For suburban or country dogs that may not encounter as many dogs on their daily walks, allow more time for them to get to know each other—one to two minutes or longer if they are showing an active interest in each other.

MEET-UP TIPS: If you live in an area where the dog population is limited, consider getting involved with a group socialization class in your neighborhood, e.g., at a vet's office or supervised training classes.

Note: *Always end on a good note!* If your last canine encounter was with a dog that snapped, growled or snarled, try to find another friendly dog before you return home. Last impressions count. Leave your dog wanting more good canine rendezvous.

When dogs and owners connect, be sure to exchange contact information so you can arrange for doggy playdates.

ACE STUDENTS

John attended every session, followed it to the letter and got results. Legs's increased tailgating opportunities brought out a hardworking canine-ality that complemented his owner's work ethic. The two gained insights into each other, thereby enhancing their cooperation training connection. Every session always ended on a good note, which instilled confidence and trust at both ends of the leash. John took the process to heart and understood that a caring commitment and tailgating needs are for the life of a dog.

John is now a genuine crossover trainer who no longer uses punishing methods to work with his dog. His techniques are positive, motivational and incentive-based. Legs's behavior is continually reinforced by his owner's adherence to a personalized program supported by ongoing tailgating.

Legs would often home-board with me when John was traveling. He turned out to be quite smart. The little guy was always asking for extra-credit tailgating assignments. The once-timid Havenese even started to tag along with Professor Sophie in her classes. At first he sat in a corner as Sophie refined the canine manners of a new group of puppies. Then during the next couple of sessions, he took on the role of teacher's assistant. Now he's advanced to the distinguished position of co-professor. The result: another academic in the Sexton household.

Tailgating Do's	Tailgating Don'ts
DO seek out lots of social opportunities with other dogs of all ages, sizes and breeds.	DON'T push your dog beyond his tolerance.
DO take different routes on walks with your dog and rotate his toys.	DON'T expose your dog to untrustworthy people or reactive dogs.

DO wear different types of clothing such as baseball caps, gloves, scarves, high heels, sneakers, etc.	DON'T mingle in areas that are unsanitary.
DO be sure to visit places where a dog is likely to encounter children.	DON'T force an encounter if your dog is pulling back.
DO seek out opportunities to be around sights, smells and sounds of daily living, such as outdoor cafés or hot dog stands.	DON'T coddle your dog when he appears frightened because you'll reinforce and reward that response. In a calm, nonreactive manner, remove him from the situation.

THREE COMMON TAILGATING QUESTIONS

Question: How often should you throw a tailgating party?

Answer: Every day and all day. Being an innovative tailgating event planner is fun and joyful as you watch your dog at any age experience new things for the first time.

Question: I have two dogs. One breezed through tailgating and the other is still having tailgating challenges. What gives?

Answer: All dogs are different. Their reactions and responses will be as unique as their abilities to learn and adapt to the world around them. Go slowly, think steady progress and have patience.

Question: Cagney, my three-year-old cocker spaniel, started barking at anyone wearing a hat. He didn't do this as a puppy. Why is he behaving this way?

Answer: Tailgating is for the life of a dog and not just for the puppyhood stage. It's normal for a dog to go through changes at different stages of his life. Didn't you go through a phase in your teens that was completely different from when you were in your twenties? Cagney needs to become reacclimated to people wearing hats. Toss a hat tailgating party and leave a bunch around the house. Whenever he goes near any of the hats, toss a treat to transform his relationship with hats into a positive one. Cagney: *"See hats and get treats. I like hats!"* When outdoors, be on the lookout for hat wearers. Spot them and redirect Cagney's focus using a treat. In one to three weeks, he'll be relaxed toward all things hats. Innovative tailgating folks may take it up a notch and seek out friends wearing a hard hat, police cap or wide-brimmed hat to work with hat-phobic dogs.

STAGES OF DEVELOPMENT

Age, environment, health and various other circumstances impact a dog's tailgating ability to learn, integrate and acclimate.

Age	Developmental Stage of Puppies
Pre-birth	Prenatal Period: Like babies, puppies can be petted prior to their birth. Studies indicate petting the mother dog before birth makes puppies more tolerant of handling.
1–3 weeks	Transitional Period: Physical changes take place. Pups need their mother for all biological functions—eating, eliminating and staying warm. Littermates play a role, and gentle human contact is encouraged. On Days 3–16 for three to four seconds daily, introduce the following: Gently rub paw pads.

	Handle the puppies in two positions: head upright, tail down; then tail up and head down. Using an ice cube or damp towel, briefly stroke the paws—this introduces mild stress for the purpose of increasing tolerance and accepting new conditions.
3–5 weeks	Primary Socialization stage: Interaction increases between mom, littermates and humans. Each day for three to four minutes: Introduce mild auditory and visual stress (turn on the television, play music, flick the lights on and off). Place the pups on a variety of surfaces. Place different objects in each pup's line of sight. Spend one-on-one time with each puppy—stroking, talking and holding.
6–12 weeks	Secondary Socialization stage: The puppies are curious and begin to explore the world around them. This is the time to get the TAILGATE PARTY into high gear! To-Do List: Get a health check. Keep all tailgating and training sessions short and sweet (ten sessions a day of two to ten minutes—avoid going beyond fifteen minutes). Tailgate and train in lots of different locations and on various surfaces, since dogs have limited generalization skills. Sensibly expose the pups to people of all sizes and appearances. Add sounds, sights and everyday situations into their routines. At eight weeks of age, enroll them in puppy socialization class with other healthy dogs of different breeds and sizes.

Age	Developmental Stage of Puppies
	Involve all family members in tailgating and training. Benefits of Tailgating: Stimulates the development of the brain and immune system. Helps build the ability to analyze situations—Fido: *"I've seen uniformed people. Nothing scary about them."* Note: At eight weeks some puppies go through a fearful phase. If this happens, don't get overly cautious. Become more of an inspired leader by encouraging them to make positive associations with anything that causes them to back away or act scared.
13–16 weeks	Continue Tailgating: Add distractions and sounds like thunder, hammering, knocking, etc. Puppy teething takes place between twelve and twenty weeks and can be painful. Be sure to have plenty of chew toys available and don't be concerned if you notice blood, as this can be quite normal. Look inside their mouth to make sure the baby teeth are not blocking any of the adult teeth. Other Things: Arrange playdates with other dogs. Sit in the lobby, driveway or on the front porch with your puppy. Acclimate him to your lifestyle. Example: If you travel a great deal, get him desensitized to seeing a suitcase. Note: At four months old, some puppies go through an avoidance phase similar to when they were eight weeks old. Step up the tailgating. Don't let a pup fall behind the learning curve.

17–20 weeks	Maturation Phase: Six to sixteen weeks is the most impressionable age for a puppy. Some dogs mature later than others. For those pups, review the recommendations for 13–16 weeks. For others, they will now be entering adolescence. Expect them, like a typical teenager, to test you. Go full throttle on the tailgating and work on commands to keep them occupied and focused on behavior you want to reinforce.
	Other Things:
	Schedule their last series of vaccination shots.
	If you're planning to spay or neuter, this is the right time.
	Adult teeth are coming in, so provide a bone to chew.

BYE-BYE, PUPPYHOOD

Though I emphasize "early" socialization, it's critical to understand that tailgating is a lifelong endeavor. Don't be surprised if, in a few months or a year, you notice an increase in unwanted behavior. Step up the tailgating. An adolescent dog might begin to test an owner as the pooch grows into his adult body and assimilates to his environment. No two dogs are alike and all go through various life stages in unique ways. Many enter a period of "terrible twos" where they challenge owners, seek greater independence or become reactive. Canine health issues or lifestyle changes in a household may also impact behavior. Take stock of your particular situation and don't rule out a visit to the vet. If any problems persist, don't hesitate to go back to square one with training. Never stop learning.

Age	Developmental Stage of Adolescent and Adult Dogs
5–12 months	Puppy is now an adolescent and full of high jinks and energy. In the wild, this would be the time that he'd begin to hunt. He'll be looking around and doing lots of exploring. He may become more defiant and begin to challenge your leadership. All his adult teeth should be in. (Review chapter 5, "Bite Inhibition 101" section, p. 96.)
1 year–18 months	During this young adult stage, a dog becomes more set in his ways but still can tailgate with the best of them. Don't stop the party. Get more creative and consider enrolling him in a Canine Good Citizen Program and have him graduate to a therapy dog. LINKS: Canine Good Citizenship Program http://www.akc.org/events/cgc/program.cfm Delta Society (Therapy Dog) http://www.deltasociety.org/
19 months–4 years	Anticipate resistance to new things if tailgate parties have become less frequent. Some dogs go through a random cycle of fear-based behavior. Watch for signs of canine stress or anxiety. If you detect any, reestablish tailgating activities. Also, consider: Day care that is reputable. Owners should do research, ask for references and spot-check to ensure consistent care is being provided. The use of dog walkers to increase exposure to different people and get more exercise. Ignoring the warning signs of an under-socialized dog can bring heartbreak. It can even be dangerous. Owners' calls to trainers spike around this period. There's confusion as to why their dogs suddenly have become reactive and aggressive.

"He was such a great puppy. I never had a problem, and then all of a sudden . . ." This is known as ALL-OF-A-SUDDEN SYNDROME. Of course it's not usually "all of a sudden." It's often because canine behavior issues have been overlooked or misread. (Review "Canine Speak," p. 11.)

Recommendations for ALL-OF-A-SUDDEN SYNDROME:

Go into Sherlock Canine Holmes mode and consider:

Have his tailgate exposures been limited? If the answer is yes, remember that dogs don't generalize their behavior the way we do. They need continual lifetime exposures. It takes lots of repetitions for a dog's memory to build associations with and reliable behavior to stimuli. A lapse in exposure will result in a decrease in wanted or reliable behavior.

Did lunging at other dogs happen all of a sudden, or was displacement behavior such as licking, head turning and snarling overlooked?

Have there been recent life changes, such as a new baby or a new job with longer hours? How about a change in diet? Has health declined for either owner or dog? These are common causes of canine behavioral changes.

Rebooting tailgating dynamics often resolves 911 canine behavior emergency issues.

5–7 years	Socializing a dog at this stage is more challenging. He's become *more* set in his ways, so consistent and repetitive tailgating is of utmost importance. While it may be a slower process, you can still get his tailgating groove back on.
	Celebrate even if your dog ends up making only one new dog pal, or simply becomes a darling to the morning doorman.
	Turn tailgating into an interactive and rewarding game. Older dogs, like older people, get set in their ways and establish habits, but adjusting to new situations, people and other dogs is still possible through tailgating.

Age	Developmental Stage of Adolescent and Adult Dogs
8–15 years	Many older rescue dogs demonstrate a "bring it on" attitude when it comes to tailgating. The once sedate older pooch can rekindle his puppyhood and reconnect with it. For physical and mental reasons, exercise is important at every stage of a dog's life. However, never force a dog into an activity if he exhibits, or you suspect, pain.

FIVE FUN TAILGATING ACTIVITIES

1. Take your dog to the bank to meet people.
2. Sit in your lobby or on the front stoop of your building.
3. Take your pooch to the Laundromat while you do your laundry.
4. Shop at pet-friendly stores.
5. Supply those wearing uniforms with treats to give to your dog.

Tailgating is the motivating, user-friendly concept that links everyday experiences with training opportunities. It can be as simple as sitting on a park bench and watching the world go by—a tailgating technique that's perfect for all dogs, especially the sensitive ones.

TAILGATING TESTIMONIAL

"The tailgating techniques have been miraculous for Legs," John explained. "He's a dog you'd feel comfortable allowing in crowds large and small. There are times when I have to teach for a couple of hours. I can bring Legs, and he's comfortable. I can also bring him to a reception with a few hundred students. Legs won't be overwhelmed in any of these circumstances. He'll walk around and students will be startled to see a dog, but he won't bark or growl at them, though he might lick them. If they fuss over him, that won't upset him, it will delight him. When children come over to us while we're on the ferry to Fire Island, I don't have to worry that he's going to bite or scare them. He's comfortable and confident with himself and with our lifestyle. And he enjoys sitting with me to watch a baseball game."

Chain of Commands

Commands are the guardrails that guide dogs toward good behavior while curbing and managing their canine drives. Once mastered, they become the invisible leashes that provide all dogs with more social opportunities. Commands make behavior reliable as well as easy to accomplish. Studies have shown that dogs can be taught up to 140 commands. Of course that depends on a dog's learning aptitude and the training commitment an owner is willing to make. This chapter concentrates on three commands that can become lifesaving: LEAVE IT, COME and STAY.

Communication should begin with training basic obedience. This establishes a dialogue and a bonding opportunity between owners and dogs. LEAVE IT, combined with LOOK-AT-ME, can convert a squirrel-obsessed pooch that's challenging to walk into an owner-infatuated dog. A dog following your instructions to ignore the distraction of the squirrel with a LEAVE IT and then being REDIRECTED (told what to do) with

LOOK-AT-ME is so much easier to manage than if you had to struggle and forcefully restrain him. In order to achieve desired and reliable results, however, you also have to do the work.

SAFETY

Safety is another important reason owners need to become proficient with their chain of commands. If the lifesaving commands COME and STAY aren't reliable, then the dog racing across a street after a squirrel or a ball puts two or more lives in jeopardy. Countless owners have been seriously injured or even died trying to rescue their pets in such situations.

"When I made the decision to get a dog, my friends kept telling me, 'You're going to have to walk her,'" said Roxanne. "Did they think I couldn't pick up poop? Then they added, 'At least three walks a day.' Looking back, I now understand that I didn't realize what walking my dog Sadie would involve. Other owners can juggle phone calls, text and shop while their dog struts alongside as a perfect canine companion, but that wasn't me."

Sadie, an eight-week-old, dappled mini-dachshund, was a regular at the emergency vet clinic. Giardia, a parasitic intestinal infection that triggers diarrhea and

Sadie's owner applies user-friendly commands to gain her dog's cooperation and ensure her safety.

vomiting, was the repeated diagnosis. On her last visit she came close to dying. However, her ailments did not deter her from being a professional scavenger. Outdoors she would become a high-powered vacuum cleaner with the maneuvering and agility of an Olympic athlete. Her sport of choice was the collaring of rotting, teensy pieces of five-day-old hamburger, turkey or other decaying food.

Roxanne had lost confidence in her ability to train Sadie. Too many unnerving hours had been spent in the vet's waiting room hoping to hear, "She's going to be okay this time." But what about next time? And when would that "next time" be? Soon "next times" started to feel like daily occurrences and Roxanne was becoming paralyzed just thinking about walking her dog outside. Keeping Sadie alive would require effectively curbing and controlling her instinctive impulses (prey drive).

"Walking Sadie was scary. It made me paranoid. How to best train her circled my thoughts. I was militant, but simply outmatched and exhausted. My diminishing finances from hefty vet bills combined with seesawing emotions of self-doubt and guilt left me questioning if I was even the right guardian for this dog. Sadie's life depended on my attentive, focused and vigilant street awareness. My friends' warnings about walking her at least three times a day echoed painfully in my thoughts. I now realized that I knew very little about what was involved in walking a dog."

BASIC TRAINING

Roxanne isn't alone in underestimating the complexities of dog walking. The missing dynamic between Roxanne and Sadie was BASIC training: Be Affirming Securing Impulse Control. With BASIC, or lifesaving commands, owners must be affirming in order to build and secure their dogs' impulse control. It aligns with my training motto: "Lead with communication." Commit to telling a dog what to do and what not to do with consistency and repetition.

BASIC training coordinates the distinctive canine impulses with what influences and drives dog behavior (canine triggers, environment, lifestyle). It then crafts and further modifies a tailor-made training program for each owner and dog.

The aim is to motivate dogs to have patience and manners. The reward system develops a canine mind-set capable of associating good behaviors with positive consequences based on a learn-to-earn model. Incentive comes in the form of treats, praise, a trip to the dog run or being out and about with the owner. Like children, dogs learn to think twice before reacting with unwanted behavior that won't be rewarded.

SADIE SNAPSHOT

Like all dogs, Sadie was born without behavioral impulse control. A forager, she operated off her prey drive. Her impulse was to use her senses of smell and taste to search out and conquer all scraps, tidbits and morsels. The prey drive for her was a powerful force connected to her genetics. It also generated an activity that she found rewarding. Her party-girl canine-ality was best suited to the type of training that adds a touch of entertainment to each command.

With Sadie, I suggested that Roxanne use LOOK-AT-ME as though she were playing peekaboo with an infant. Motivated by the fun and interactive game, Sadie offered her attention. She loves merrymaking and this game aligned with her party animal learning style. Putting the festivities into Sadie's training techniques did more than get her to look up at Roxanne. They were the start of controlling her impulse behavior.

When I pass a chocolate store, I'm tempted to go in, but I can control my impulse. Sadie has less restraint and she's wired with *"gotta-do"* energy. She needed a firm LEAVE IT command. The training goal was to make checking (LEAVE IT) with Roxanne more rewarding than vacuuming the sidewalks for curbside scraps.

SOME CANINE IMPULSES THAT NEED CURBING

- Inappropriate greetings, e.g., jumping on or barking at guests
- Charging out the front door
- Begging for food
- Not coming when called
- Reacting to other dogs while on-leash
- Pushy/controlling behavior
- Pulling, not walking, on lead
- Chewing furniture
- Growling around the food bowl
- Excessive barking
- Scavenging

COMMAND DO's	COMMAND DON'Ts
DO use a calm and confident tone of voice.	DON'T use a questioning or pleading tone to give a command.
DO say the command only once.	DON'T change a command midway.
DO be consistent and specific with commands.	DON'T use physical force, e.g., push butt down or hold in position.

KATE'S SEVEN TRAINING MANTRAS

1. Begin training with the leash on your dog. This is to maintain control and prevent a dog from wandering off. Stepping on the leash enables hands-free authority and takes away the reflexive action of pulling at both ends of the leash.

2. Training sessions should begin indoors without distractions. Once mastered, add distractions and more challenging locations, e.g., a park or the lobby.

3. After a command is given, see if your dog can hold the position for one or two seconds, then mark with "YES" and praise and treat. The association with the command will become more meaningful to a dog.

4. Keep a relaxed and upright body position. Once a command becomes reliable, be innovative with your directive technique. This can be achieved by altering your body stances.

5. Train in lots of locations and incrementally increase the physical distance between you and your dog every other repetition once reliable results are achieved. This cultivates a resilient dog with increased social opportunities for both ends of the leash—and addresses a dog's limited ability to generalize behavior in a variety of locations and situations.

6. Take a break between a series of commands. Training and play/exercise activities are *"GOTTA GO" MOTIVATORS* (p. 109). Breaks keep a dog and owner focused and refreshed. It's best to be short and sweet with the training to achieve positive results.

7. Be sure to end the training session on a good note with a JACKPOT.

Once a dog has a reliable command, begin delaying the reward. Training shouldn't create a dependency on treats (BRIBE). They're used in the beginning as motivators and then as occasional rewards.

Commanding Techniques and Terms Associated with Chain of Commands

TECHNIQUE	PURPOSE
LURING	Hand-guide a dog with a treat or toy as you initiate a behavior.
	High-value treats entice a dog to use his nose to follow an owner's hand into a desired position.
SHAPING	Break down the behavior into incremental stages. For example, a play bow is a half-down position. Mark and reward to help the dog want to, then slide all the way down.
	Shaping is accomplished by using the marker signal "YES" to mark and reinforce each incremental stage of learning. For example, the kids' hot, warm or cold game. Hot = very close, cold = not close at all. So, "YES" and treat on the half-down, no marker or treat if not achieving desired position.
CAPTURING	Mark canine behavior as it happens spontaneously, e.g.: a dog lies down by your feet when you watch TV. As he lies down you say, "YES," thereby marking desired impromptu behavior. Follow with treat and praise.

LEAVE IT—MEAN IT

Roxanne's commands were given in a reserved manner. Sadie couldn't hear LEAVE IT in the way it was needed. This dog demanded an owner's firm, self-assured tone without a hint of "maybe." The way to convey this to Roxanne was to show, not tell, her. LEAVE IT, and all commands addressed in a self-assured manner, interrupt a dog's behavior.

LEAVE IT needed to be punched out as a purposeful directive heard by Sadie. I worked the commands indoors with Roxanne and Sadie until they became reliable and then took the session outdoors. Personal coaching made the difference and built up Roxanne's confidence. Sadie could hear LEAVE IT spoken as: LEAVE IT—MEAN IT. This delivered results.

FEATURED TRAINING TECHNIQUE: LEAVE IT

Quick Description: LEAVE IT

LEAVE IT tells a dog: "Don't put that in your mouth," or lets him know to ignore a particular distraction.

LEAVE IT goes against a dog's instinctual prey drive, which can include:

- Chasing moving objects or animals (skateboards, scooters, squirrels, pigeons, blowing leaves)
- Vacuuming the sidewalks (scavenging) for scraps and morsels (chicken bones, pizza crusts, feces, cigarette butts)
- Curbing a dog from lunging at other dogs or objects (baby stroller, wheelchair)

LEAVE IT is also for inside the home when there's an irresistible turkey dinner on the counter, a handy remote control, a hamster out of his cage or an ibuprofen pill loose on the floor.

LEAVE IT Steps—Part 1

1. Kneel next to your dog and place a yummy treat inside your closed fist that's placed on the floor. (For this exercise, use dehydrated

chicken strips or other high-value treats that don't crumble. Also have some within reach of your other hand.)

2. Expect him to sniff, paw and lick to get the treat. Wait for him to pause or lose interest in going after the treat. At that moment, immediately mark "YES" and quickly treat him with the other hand. The goal is for him to make the association that his pause (LEAVE IT) earns him the reward.

3. Repeat steps 1 and 2 for ten repetitions. For each LEAVE IT response, move your fist with the treat to a different area of the floor. At this point, he should start pausing more frequently.

4. After a few successful repetitions with the dog reliably "pausing," begin to open your fist and reveal the treat. Chances are he'll attempt to get the food again. If he does, quickly close your fist and wait for him to "pause." Slowly open your hand, revealing the treat. If he pauses, say, "YES," and treat from your other hand with a JACKPOT. Now continue to let the dog see the treat in your hand and wait for him to LEAVE IT, then reward with the other hand, occasionally adding a JACKPOT REWARD. Repeat for ten reliable repetitions.

LEAVE IT Steps—Part 2 (Adding the Command Language)

1. Advance to putting the treat on the floor with your hand in a cupped position over the treat. Move your hand away from the treat. If the dog pauses and doesn't go for the treat, mark "YES" and treat from a different location with JACKPOT REWARDS. Repeat this step ten times.

Note: If he goes for the treat, then revert to covering the food until he leaves the treat alone on the floor and pauses until you treat him from another location.

2. If he's responding reliably to the concept of "leaving it," change to a standing position and place a dehydrated chicken treat under your foot. Repeat the earlier steps but this time lift your foot away from the treat. When he pauses with you in a standing position, mark "YES" and treat from a different location with JACKPOT REWARDS. Repeat this step ten times.

3. The nonverbal LEAVE IT pause should be for two or three seconds before marking "YES."

4. Once you are in a standing position and a reliable pause from the dog has been established, start adding the command language. "LEAVE IT" should be commanded with an authoritative tone. Say, "LEAVE IT," every time the dog pauses to create an association with the verbal command and his PAUSE behavior. The JACKPOT REWARDS will have become a strong motivator for the dog to start looking up at you when he pauses. The dog will be conditioned to understand that it's more rewarding to LEAVE IT (chicken bones, shoe, garbage) and to check in with you.

Note: The message is that if he sees it and LEAVES IT, better things happen.

SADIE'S UNEDITED TRANSCRIPT

With me as a translator, Sadie had a few words of advice for Roxanne as well:

- *I'm quite willing to carry out commands. The ground rule is: Be decisive and clear by telling me and teaching me what you want me to do.*
- *Okay, I admit to being the party animal canine-ality type. So I suggest the following: (1) Use a consistent and playful voice when commanding. (2) Realize that because I like to party I'm easily distracted.*

Once unable to resist food scraps on the street, Sadie now does,
thanks to the LEAVE IT command.

I'm looking for excitement and that can come from finding curbside morsels. To counter foraging behavior, keep LOOK-AT-ME and LEAVE IT commands coming. I'm conscious about my waistline so surprise me with rewards like praise, not just treats. (3) Oh, I also might need more rehearsal time to ensure that my commands are reliable. I'm all about the party so expect rehearsals to be fun.

- *The fear you have about taking me for walks can be managed. Start by changing my equipment. Use a gentle leader. I'm willing to wear a basket muzzle (p. 178) until the LEAVE IT command becomes reliable. The word on basket muzzles is that they're not for punishment. They're management tools.*

- *Be vigilant with the LEAVE IT command. Speak it to capture and motivate my behavior into the bigger reward of our bonding time. LEAVE IT must signify that I should completely ignore a distraction. It should also convey "Better things happen when I check in with you." Incentive-based training produces results.*

- *Let's get to the root of my scavenging behavior. I do it because it's fun. My scavenging is like a girl who loves to shop. Let's work the GO-FIND-IT game into training so that I can safely scavenge indoors on cue and be entertained while exercising.*
- *Playtime (you can keep calling it training) is when we work on our connection and become innovative with our techniques. GO-FIND-IT (toss me a treat at a distance and then command, "GO-FIND-IT") can advance to HIDE & SEEK (hide treats around the house, behind doors, under my bed or in the guest room and command, "GO SEEK"). Both games help me to understand that scavenging is acceptable when done with permission.*
- *You're not doing anything wrong. Neither am I. We simply need to work together and be consistent with our training system. I'll go in the direction you guide me. Please lead the way for us to build trust in each other.*

QUICK EXTRA COMMAND GUIDELINES

1. Set your dog up for success.
   - Work slowly and incrementally.
   - If you are not getting the desired behavior with a single command, break it down into smaller segments.
   - Be aware of your timing and coordination.
   - Be observant of Canine Speak (p. 11). A dog that yawns, turns his head or wags his tail is communicating. He might be unsure, confused or just eager to learn.
2. Be quick to mark the dog that performs the right behavior.
   - When a dog responds with the right commanded behavior, it's critical to immediately mark and reward him.

- "YES" is a good marker signal that lets a dog know he's done something right. Be consistent with your marker signal cue word.

3. Make sure your dog is behaving on your, not his, terms.

   - If commanded to SIT and a dog lies down, don't reward him. Instead, provide a consequence. Use a no-reward tone of EH-EH! and turn away for five seconds. Then repeat the command and if he SITS, mark "YES" and reward with JACKPOT treats.

   - Dogs, like kids, will test to see what they can get away with.

CANINE MANNERS

Dogs need to have good manners. Like social skills, basic obedience is learned behavior. Over time, dogs require less cueing for the commands or redirects because the behavior becomes ingrained and habituated. Teaching my son to share his toys, eat with his mouth closed and brush his teeth after meals are my responsibilities as a parent. Eventually I won't have to tell him to do these things because he will understand that this behavioral etiquette is expected of him. Of course, especially with brushing his teeth, there are occasions to remind him.

Our role as dog guardians is to provide lifelong social and behavioral skills. Commands, along with proper socialization, are training mechanisms that add a level of canine civility into the mix. These commands cultivate a dog that can be taken anywhere and everywhere because he has agreeable social graces. Those without chain of commands training have a difficult time getting out and about. The tendency will be to leave them at home. Sadly, if a dog's manners escalate to an unacceptable level, or one where aggression is involved, many owners consider surrendering the pet to a shelter.

Effective impulse control develops canine patience. It gets a dog to think twice before acting. Putting a dog in SIT-STAY before offering anything (dinner, a toy, a bone) teaches manners. Think of SIT- STAY as the "please," "may I?" and "thank you" of canine behavioral response.

TWO OTHER LIFESAVING COMMANDS

COME and STAY, like LEAVE IT, represent guardian commands that protect a dog while he's being responsive to his owner's authority. Teaching a dog lifesaving commands is similar to parents instructing children to cross streets carefully, be mindful around hot surfaces and play in safe areas. A dog's welfare is dependent on an owner being affirming in securing impulse control.

FEATURED TRAINING TECHNIQUE: COME

Quick Description: COME

COME commands a dog to go to his owner when called. It shouldn't be a suggestion but a self-assured directive stating, "NOW."

COME should never be associated with punishment. This will defeat the purpose of the command for owner and dog.

> The dog off-leash in a park, on the beach, in building hallways, the woods or the backyard must be trained to have reflexive conditioning to the COME command.
>
> GOAL: COME must capture a dog's complete attention and always be reflexive and rewarding.

COME Steps

1. Place your dog in a SIT-STAY if that's a reliable behavior, or have someone hold your dog on a leash. Next, show the dog a yummy-smelling high-value treat, then walk four to six feet away.

2. Call your dog's name once with a happy tone to get his attention. Then move your arm down with the open palm of your hand facing him (the same physical gesture as TOUCH TARGET, p. 31) while enthusiastically commanding, "COME."

3. Once the dog comes to you, gently take hold of his collar from under the muzzle, mark with "YES" and treat from the other hand. The goal of this step is to create acceptance of having his collar touched without him squirming or displaying discomfort.

4. Repeat steps 1–3 for ten repetitions. The sequence is: first call dog's name, then command COME, and as he nears, gently reach for and hold collar while marking "YES" and treat. "YES" conveys to a dog "job done" and serves as a release cue.

5. Once you have a reliable COME, practice the command in a different location in your home. Increase the distance with each repetition. Include DELAY REWARDS and start adding JACKPOT REWARDS for faster responses. Do this for ten repetitions.

6. Once COME is reliable indoors, take it outdoors and repeat the above sequence. When outdoors, train this command with him on an extra-long leash. Use high-value treats to keep him motivated.

Puppies love to follow their owners so be sure to take advantage of this. When a pup follows after you, practice the command COME and make sure to gently introduce reaching for the collar. Include praising and treating as you do this. Turn COME into a pleasurable, reflexive behavior that's fun to do for you and your pooch.

For Ollie and all dogs, COME needs to be established as
a reflexive and reliable command.

FEATURED TRAINING TECHNIQUE: STAY

Quick Description: STAY

STAY is the "MUST HALT" command that keeps a dog from moving. It lets a dog know he needs to relax until released from the command.

At street corners, waiting for elevators or whenever there's a need to limit a dog's movement; STAY is the command that tells a dog to be patient, polite and attentive.

For exuberant canine greeters that overwhelm guests coming into your home or elsewhere (e.g., elevators), STAY and SIT-STAY establish welcoming well-behaved manners.

GOAL: STAY communicates to a dog "STOP and relax in a comfortable place" and wait for the release cue "OK."

The STAY command can be used in combination with SIT, DOWN and STAND. It serves to encourage patience and can be used to secure a dog's safety.

STAY Steps

1. Command SIT or DOWN, whichever is the more reliable behavior for your dog.

2. Show the palm of your hand with fingers upward (like a stop sign). It's very important to use a decisive hand signal before you command STAY. Hold your hand "stop sign" in front of your dog

for two seconds, conveying, "Don't move," before saying, "OK" (release cue, telling your dog the task is complete). Then praise and give him a treat. Do five repetitions for two- to three-second STAYs, then advance to ten repetitions, adding a few more seconds per repetition. The goal is to increase the length of the STAY.

Note: If the dog doesn't get up on the "OK" release cue, use the TOUCH TARGET hand gesture after the "OK" (release cue) to encourage him to come out of the STAY position.

3. Once getting ten-second STAYs has become reliable, continue to SIT-STAY for fifteen, then twenty seconds. Work in the increased time increments gradually. The goal is to achieve reliable thirty-second SIT-STAYs. Give bigger JACKPOTS for the longer STAYs, and less for the shorter ones.

4. If your dog gets up prior to being RELEASED, make a negative interruptive sound like "EH-EH." Then turn your back on him for three seconds. Start over and reduce the amount of time for the STAY. Keeping a dog motivated is crucial for achieving success with this command.

5. Once the dog has achieved reliable thirty-second STAYs in many locations, practice by adding distance. Take two steps back and then say the "OK" release cue. This will teach a DISTANT STAY command. Like with the increased amount of time, the DISTANT STAY command is about gradually increasing the distance from the dog as he remains in a SIT-STAY command.

Practice SIT-STAY in different locations in your home. Add JACKPOT REWARDS for longer DISTANT STAYs and less for short ones. Each step needs to be mastered before progressing to longer-distance STAY commands.

Note: DOWN is often a more comfortable position for a dog for longer periods of "wait" time. If you feel a dog is becoming less responsive to STAY, take a break and restart the session using the DOWN command.

> To strengthen the STAY command, work it into play sessions. If you're playing fetch with a ball, try commanding STAY on a toss. This will help build safety behavior when outdoors or in other tricky situations requiring controlled behavior.

ONE COMMAND AT A TIME

Mastering one command at a time (isolating commands) is necessary in order to achieve results. Learning the grammar and punctuation of owner-canine command training language leads to an intrinsic bond where owner and dog learn to anticipate each other and work as a pair. Think of it as being able to finish each other's sentences because there's a familiarity, a recognizable pattern of behavior and a desire to interact with each other.

Dogs don't reason the same way we do, but they constantly observe us and pick up on our energy and body language. If owners have patience and spend sufficient time training with them, dogs will eventually reflect their lifestyles and align with their habits. If I open the closet where Sophie's leash is located, without commanding she'll scurry over and place herself in a SIT (good behavior) because that action lets her know there's a potential for a walk. However, if my son's toys, not her leash, are taken out of the closet, she understands "no walk" and she's likely to return to her bed.

TRAINING TECHNIQUES SPECIFIC TO SADIE AND ROXANNE

Sadie's *"DIRECTOR, PLEASE"* learning style called for Roxanne to definitively tell her what to do. The challenge was that this dachshund has a highly developed instinctual prey drive that lives to scavenge. After testing her on several commands, I was able to make an assessment regarding compliance, resistance and her ability to focus. Her spot-on timing, execution and eagerness to learn was matched with a sweetness that said, *"Let's party on some more."* She was a director's dream. She wanted a cue line (LEAVE IT, spoken as LEAVE IT—MEAN IT), after which she raced to hit her mark in order to hear "GOOD GIRL" and receive a treat. Sadie had no intention of costing the studio money, meaning Roxanne would no longer be facing emergency vet bills.

Roxanne is representative of many owners I work with. Her confidence needed boosting and her bond with her dog required reengineering. The relationships are often in a delicate place that feels hopeless, but isn't. Deep inside, these owners have what it takes to become the best trainers for their dogs. Whenever I encounter these situations, I ask the owners to show me how they're commanding behavior. Their voices and body postures tell me much of what I need to know. In Sadie's case, I recommended a basket muzzle for Sadie until Roxanne became more self-assured in giving commands.

Roxanne was not comfortable with my suggestion of using a basket muzzle. The public perception of a dog wearing a basket muzzle is that the dog is aggressive, dangerous and uncontrollable, and that the owner is uncaring for not taking the time to train the dog. However, trainers understand that a basket muzzle is a lifesaving, last-resort tool to be used only during an interim training period for this type of dog. Owners who use this equipment are caring and responsible. Many owners who use this equipment are working toward establishing reliability with LEAVE IT and DROP IT commands.

Roxanne's decision not to use the muzzle for Sadie was a personal choice. It came with the knowledge that she'd have to be extremely vigilant and firm with her commands. For others, the equipment might serve as support and provide the owner with ample opportunity to secure the LEAVE IT command. The role of a trainer is to be understanding and able to gauge an owner's ability. We are coaches, not judges. In this case, Roxanne stepped up and did what was required for her dog.

> Commands help a dog figure out what his owner wants from him, which enables the owner to channel the dog's attention toward desired canine behavior.

BASKET MUZZLES

Basket muzzles are not used exclusively for aggression. Living with the "bad dog" stereotype image is better than risking a dog's life. A child who wears braces is not being punished. Likewise, though not used to alter physical appearance, a muzzle helps straighten out impulse behavior, and is also a temporary tool.

In cases involving an aggressive dog that's a danger to people or other dogs, I strongly object to an owner who decides to overlook doing what's necessary to ensure public safety. Dog aggression indoors or outdoors has to be properly managed. No exceptions made. Explaining the training options, benefits and drawbacks is always important. A muzzle shows that an owner understands and honors his dog's behavior.

INTRODUCING A BASKET MUZZLE TO A DOG

1. Place cream cheese on the interior of the muzzle. This will motivate him to stick his nose through to reach the treat. Let him lick the cream cheese. Repeat this step five to ten times or until the behavior becomes fun and reflexive for him.

2. Clip the straps loosely behind his ears and continue to let him lick the cream cheese for one minute. Then take it off and hide it from him for ten seconds.

A basket muzzle enables a dog to have its mouth open and relaxed.

3. Repeat step 1, but this time comfortably secure the muzzle with the straps having a one-finger-width fit. Distract him with an action he enjoys, such as petting or brushing. The emphasis should be less on reinforcing him with treats and more on his becoming blasé about wearing the muzzle (desensitization).

4. Leash him up and walk around the house. Place him in a SIT and reward him by sliding treats through the sides of the basket muzzle. Dehydrated chicken strips will do the trick (counterconditioning).

5. Once you feel he's acclimated to the basket muzzle, take him outdoors and continue to keep the commands and treats coming. Check the straps to make sure of the fit.

6. Be sure to give him affection, belly rubs or a game of chase with the

muzzle on to speed up his acceptance of the equipment. Letting him perform activities he enjoys with the muzzle on creates positive associations.

NO QUICK FIXES

Quick fixes do not realistically resolve unwanted canine behavior. You may need to manage a situation—such as holding a dog back from chasing after a squirrel—but that in itself will not cause a permanent behavior change since the world is filled with squirrels and other canine triggers. Learned commands direct a dog to get where he needs to go in life with his owner.

TRAINING IS BUILT ON TRUST

A chain of commands links owners and dogs as partners and companions. The responsiveness to owners comes about because the reward system evolves from a bond built on trust, support and encouragement. Treats are motivators, but long-term success happens because a dog is inspired to follow nurturing and insightful leadership.

"I had to change my attitude in order to train Sadie," said Roxanne. "I had to realize who she was and what she could do. Getting over my fear of walking her began with changing my thinking. I had to realize that I could do it. My initial instincts were that if I could immediately train Sadie, then everything would be easier. Kate made me understand that my instincts were just fine. I became aware that there are no quick fixes with training. It doesn't happen immediately. That was my 'aha moment.' Sadie really knows herself and has no self-esteem issues. She's happy all the time. I now get that. A part of me was scared that I would mess up. Sadie's taught me to have more trust in myself."

Chain of Command Summary

- Commit to the training process.
- Develop a training schedule that works with your lifestyle.
- Master each command in at least ten different locations.

Owners should take advantage of feeding times as "opportunistic and user-friendly" training sessions. A dog earns his meal while he's motivated and rewarded for being responsive to commands.

My dog Sophie seamlessly demonstrates that after mastering and then linking the commands SIT, DOWN, STAY and COME, dogs are ready for more advanced behavior training. Owners in my classes enjoy seeing Sophie put commands together in sequence (chaining). She puts on an entertaining show, caps it off with a spin and ends in a sit that encourages applause. These tricks helped land her a featured role in a Juicy Crittoure commercial for dog shampoo and conditioner. They're also the same skills and behavior needed every day for waiting at street corners (STAY), leaving a street morsel alone (LEAVE IT) and responding to me when I ask her for attention (LOOK-AT-ME). The goal is to build up a repertoire of commands that can be applied anytime, anywhere.

The Anxious Dog

nxious canine behavior can be upsetting, alarming and even
frightening to anyone who witnesses it. In most cases, fear is
driving the behavior and can be both apprehensive and reactionary where a dog reverts to protecting and defending himself. The fear
can relate to the proximity of an object, person, sound or situation. Anxiety is particular to each dog. Treatment plans vary and depend on the
level of intensity of their fears.

Anxiety can be caused by real or imagined threats. Here are some
examples:

- Low Level: Daisy's owner noticed that when he reached over her
  head for something that she'd tremble.
- Backstory: She's a re-homed pooch mistreated by her previous
  owner.
- Mild to Moderate: Coco, an Afghan hound, tucks her tail between

her legs and pulls her ears back whenever she spots dachshunds. If a dachshund comes over to make contact with her, Coco hides behind her owner and growls.

- Backstory: When Coco was ten weeks old a dachshund attacked her. Since that time she's been afraid of that breed or those of similar stature.
- Extreme: A dog named Annie is unable to go outside. The mere sight of her collar and leash turns her into a basket case. She hides underneath her owner's bed, overwhelmed and unable to cope.
- Backstory: Annie's primary source of fear is unknown. Did something traumatic happen to her outdoors? Is it genetics? Or is it something else?

TYPES OF ANXIETY

The four most common anxious behaviors I encounter are:

Anxiety	Manifestation
Social	Fear of people, places and things, usually due to lack of early socialization, a traumatic experience or abuse. Over time the fear becomes learned (habit) or is triggered by the presence of something unfamiliar.
Separation	Stressful and reactive behavior when left alone. Possible causes: genetics, changes in a dog's or owner's routine, relocation to a new home, a newborn child, the death of a family member or a rescue with unresolved issues.
Noise	Sensitivity to loud or unfamiliar sounds (sirens, garbage trucks, knocking on a door, cell phone ring). Fear triggered by children screaming, etc.

Anxiety	Manifestation
Environment	Fear of stairs, thresholds, elevators, a new crate, etc.
	Thunder, lightning and rain.

CALLING THE SUPERINTENDENT

One owner's dog expressed her anxiety by barking high-pitched squeals that sounded like a pig. I observed this dog spinning uncontrollably, throwing herself at the front door and snort-sneezing like a bull getting ready to charge. If you're unaware of subtle behavior differences or degrees of severity, or if you don't know what to look for or focus on, this anxiety could appear extreme or hopeless, or even be perceived as aggressive behavior. My experience as a trainer and a mother recognized this as a tantrum as opposed to an extreme case of separation anxiety. This pooch was declaring—alas, demanding—*"I can't handle you leaving me alone. I simply won't have it.* No! NO! *NO!"*

This spinning, barking and snort-sneezer would transfer her front-door anxiety—*"I don't want you to leave me alone"*—to the shower stall door. While taking a shower, the owner had to witness her dog ramming herself into the glass door, or perfecting her pig squealing and circle-spins. Neighbors, concerned and disturbed by the disconcerting noise and commotion from her apartment, reported her to the building superintendent. Looks and stares from fellow residents in the hallway and lobby let her know that they assumed I was an unfit owner. Yes, I'm talking about Sophie, my dog, Professor Sophie.

SLOW AND STEADY

With patience, understanding and time, an anxious dog can be treated and rehabilitated. Depending on the severity of the anxiety and the willingness of the owners to commit to a behavior modification plan, treatment can take as little as four weeks, or can last for months. Setbacks and regressions are to be expected since fear is a complex emotion for dogs and people. Slow and steady, one day at a time is the best approach when rehabilitating an anxious dog.

Managing Professor Sophie's low-level separation anxiety came prior to resolving it.

Anxious canine behavior may include the following:

- Panting
- Pacing
- Inability to focus
- Spinning
- Hyperactivity
- Skittishness
- Obsessive clinginess
- Cowering
- Yawning
- Blinking
- Trembling
- Lurching
- Excessive barking

- Drooling
- Dry mouth
- Smacking lips
- Lack of appetite
- Dilated eyes
- Freezing
- Whining
- Snapping
- Scratching
- Growling
- Howling
- Excessive licking or biting (e.g., paws, tail)
- Tense muscles
- Destructive chewing
- Shaking
- Sweaty paw pads
- Marking territory
- Vomiting

Review displacement behaviors and cut-off and calming signals (pp. 11–12, 14–15) for other canine behaviors that can be indicative of a dog's anxiety.

BEHAVIOR MODIFICATION PLAN

Behavior modification manages and controls a dog's emotions. The goal of a behavior modification plan is to reduce stress while changing a dog's state of mind. Desensitization and counterconditioning are the cornerstone treatments for fearful, anxious dogs. There are also extreme cases where avoidance is prescribed for a dog with significant agitation or alarming reactions to a specific trigger(s).

Note: Always rule out a medical condition before you set up a treatment plan. To best cope with their anxiety, some dogs may need psychotropic drugs prescribed by a veterinary behaviorist.

BEHAVIOR MODIFICATION TREATMENTS FOR ANXIOUS BEHAVIOR

The chart below lists several behavior modification training approaches that aid in rehabilitating and reconditioning anxious dogs. These techniques modify and manage behavior by changing a dog's association with a particular trigger—be it an object, person, sound or situation.

Treatment	Purpose
Desensitization	Build up exposure to a particular trigger in a steady and incremental process while keeping within the dog's threshold of tolerance.
Counterconditioning	Change a dog's association (mind-set) with a trigger by teaching him another behavior. Turning a negative association into a positive association by doing a commanded behavior, e.g., LOOK-AT-ME, TOUCH TARGET, SIT.
Avoidance	Avoiding a trigger is a useful way of managing behavior in the early stages of a behavior modification plan. In extreme cases of reactivity, avoidance should be implemented as much as possible.

Setting up the right treatment plan is important when you're trying to modify the behavior of an anxious dog. We want to treat the problem, not mask fearful, conditioned responses. Desensitization and counterconditioning can be used simultaneously to resolve and modify anxious behavior. Desensitization exposes a dog to reactionary triggers within his workable threshold of tolerance. Counterconditioning means redirecting a dog by giving commands (e.g., LOOK-AT-ME, SIT, DOWN) around the source of fear. It begins as soon as the dog seems at ease around the trigger (desensitization). Avoidance manages the situation.

Desensitization

Vacuum cleaners have a tendency to evoke fear in dogs. The way to make a dog less sensitive to this object and any other items or circumstances that induce fear is to let him get used to going near it. Bring it out without turning it on. Whenever he goes near it, toss treats and praise him. Allow him to get accustomed to the vacuum while it's off. Once he's accustomed to it, move it around while tossing treats to him, and gauge his response. The goal is for him not to be bothered by the motion. If he reacts by barking or cowering with his tail down, slow down, stop moving it and reengage him until he realizes that the vacuum cleaner is not a threat. An owner's JOLLY EFFECT (p. 21) and calm presence enable a puppy to compose himself and adopt a healthy and balanced threshold of tolerance.

Additional Tips for Vacuum Introduction

- Bring out the vacuum around mealtimes. The timing will encourage a pup to make a strong association with the vacuum and something good, such as his dinner.
- The added bonus of vacuuming while a pup eats is that he doesn't get underfoot as you clean.

Counterconditioning

A dog that barks at men wearing baseball caps can be taught (commanded) to LOOK-AT-ME and SIT every time a man wearing a baseball cap is spotted. The command behavior is rewarded (reinforced) with yummy high-value treats and praise. Eventually the dog associates men wearing baseball caps with a good thing that brings him praise and rewards if he performs a LOOK-AT-ME and SIT.

Avoidance

Avoidance is essential behavior modification treatment, especially if a dog's behavior is aggressive. It's a way to manage extreme cases and is advisable for owners who first need to gain mastery of their training skills. A dog lunging at people in an elevator needs his owner to practice avoidance with him in order to minimize danger to others. In a case like this, using the service elevator or taking the stairs is advisable. If you can't avoid an elevator, then step on the leash to prevent lunging and ask people not to get on the elevator with you. If a dog's fear manifests itself through aggression, or negatively impacts the quality of his life, seek qualified help right away. Learned aggression as a means of coping with anxiety and fear will be reinforced if a treatment plan is not implemented.

POTENTIAL CAUSES OF ANXIETY

Identifying the specific triggers that set off anxiety and fear may not be easy. The following can contribute to a dog's anxiety:

- Under-socialization
- Lack of exercise
- Environment
- Change in routine
- Breed and genetics
- Trauma
- Mistreatment (abuse)
- Medical condition and aging

Under-Socialization

Early socialization (tailgating) and exercise can prevent canine behavior problems. Guardians who expose pups to the world around them in responsible ways often curb shyness, timidity and aggression. The goal is to develop a canine temperament that's adaptable, confident and secure in a variety of situations and interactions. Canine fear can stem from a reaction to unfamiliar objects, people or places because dogs are often unsure how to interpret something new. Tailgating parties encourage coping and rebounding skills that reduce reactivity to triggers.

The benefit of tailgating is that it cultivates a healthy curiosity in a dog. At a young age, these pups become conditioned to tune in to their owners for understanding and comfort and for explanations about things that are strange or new to them. They'll be less reactive dogs that can go anywhere and do anything.

Exercise

Exercise, including physical and mental stimulation, is an owner's responsibility. "Exercise, exercise, exercise and socialize" is my motto for puppyhood and for the lifespan of all dogs. Tailgating and exercise are as necessary as feeding, sheltering and caring for a pooch. Studies find that exercise is the key to resolving many canine behavior issues.

Environment: "Golden Retrievers Don't Act like That"

Roscoe, a golden retriever, was fearful and skittish in the supposed comfort of his home. His behavior was becoming anxious and aggressive. He was timid, nervous and reactive to guests walking by him. His owner even remarked, "Golden retrievers don't act like that." As a general statement, that rings true, but in my line of work I've learned that any dog—

no matter what the breed—can become fearful, aggressive and even dangerous.

When I asked if anything traumatic had taken place, the owner replied, "No, nothing at all." For the next two hours I continued asking questions, working to discover and bring out Roscoe's drive and canineality. I concluded that he was bordering on being reactive, but the details the owner provided didn't add up. I was stumped.

Then I noticed that Roscoe seemed especially anxious around a group of leather storage units that kept the home clutter-free. His extra toys and leash were stored there, along with the owner's music and important files. Whenever the owner went near them, or went to get Roscoe things, the dog's behavior would heighten and he'd seem alarmed. I asked the owner about the reaction, and she said, "It's strange. He won't go near them."

I decided to improvise and take Roscoe outside to see if a change of environment would alter his behavior. As the door opened and we entered the hallway heading toward the elevator, a new Roscoe introduced himself to me. He exhibited more confidence and tenderness. He warmed up to me with happy-dog swagger and tail wagging that said, *"Come on, let's play."* That was quite a contrast from inside the apartment, where his body language had read, *"Don't you dare come near me."* It was at this time that the owner offered, "He's so unhappy in our new home."

The owner had not mentioned living in four different homes in the last two years. Roscoe was reacting to the changes in his environment. To Roscoe, the new storage units looked like the cardboard moving boxes that had accompanied each move. His heightened agitation as guests came and went was a result of his thinking that everyone was a packer and a mover.

Roscoe's anxiety and his distressing and potentially aggressive behavior were occurring because he was adjusting to yet another new home. His behavior was expressing, *"I can't relax. I need to be on guard and ready to move at a moment's notice. I don't want you near me because you might take me away from my owner's side. That's the only place that feels familiar and comforting to me. I don't want that and I will defend against that happening."* His fear and anxiety needed to be converted to a "home sweet home" spirit.

The training solution for Roscoe required the implementation of desensitizing and counterconditioning methods that included having lots of different visitors to the home. The goal was to reestablish his confidence and make him realize that visitors weren't only packers and movers. They were folks dropping over with treats and positive attention. They weren't a threat to his survival. The storage units provided an interactive game in which, on command, he'd nose-nudge certain drawers to identify where a treat could be found. They became treat dispensers, not moving boxes. They rewarded, not agitated, Roscoe.

Change in Routine: "Why Did Things Have to Change?"

Dogs dislike change. If "Exercise, exercise, exercise and socialize" is my motto, then a pooch's would be: *"Routine, routine, routine and socialize."* Routine and consistency make dogs feel secure and confident. Change can undermine a dog's stability and evoke fear. The following are some changes that can impact a dog's behavior:

- New owner(s)
- New person or pet in the house (newborn, roommate, housekeeper)
- New groomer or dog walker
- New neighbors
- Change in owner's work schedule
- Change in household (construction project, roof repair, sprinkler system installation)
- Change in feeding time
- Change in walks and outings

- Family member(s) passing away, going on vacation or leaving for college
- Companion pet passing away or being re-homed
- Rearrangement of furniture or dog crate or new floor (i.e., replacing wood floor with granite)

TRAINING TECHNIQUES SPECIFIC TO SOPHIE

Like a typical urban owner with a demanding job and complex lifestyle, my time was always limited. When Sophie first arrived at two years old, I resorted to managing her behavior by taking her to work with me. This isn't possible for everyone, nor is it the ideal solution, but it can be a management remedy in extreme cases. As things turned out, Sophie was a first-rate training assistant in my classes. Yet it was still important to increase her coping skills. Taking her everywhere wasn't something that I always wanted to do. Teaching alone time to all dogs is incredibly important because they're highly social animals that instinctually dislike being left alone or isolated. They need to be taught to accept and adapt to the realities of their owners' lifestyles.

Sophie is a Velcro dog that likes to shadow me from room to room. She is hypervigilant regarding my whereabouts. To get an idea of the level of her separation anxiety, I set up a web camera and left her alone in the apartment for thirty minutes. The footage revealed that she only squealed, barked and lunged at the front door immediately following my departure. After two to five minutes, she retired to the comfort of her bed. Her behavior was not destructive, nor did she continue to exhibit signs of pacing, panting, barking or spinning. This classified as low-level separation anxiety.

Sophie's treatment included the following:

- Desensitizing her to my departure clues
- Adding a command prior to leaving (GO TO YOUR BED)
- Adding a rewarding and time-consuming activity (Kong stuffed with yummy treats)

CHANGING DEPARTURE CUES, ADDING A COMMAND AND MAKING IT REWARDING

Often a dog becomes familiar with his owner's departure routine. He'll associate shoes, purse, backpack or briefcase with owner leaving. Owners reveal that, as they're picking out a shirt to wear or opening the sock drawer, Fluffy is already pacing, nervous, whining and jumping at their leg in distress. *"Yikes—you're leaving me!"* Is the dog a genius? Or is your routine predictable? Let's say both are true, and consider trying the following:

1. Repeat your departure routine and walk to the door but don't exit.
2. If you normally grab your keys, hat, coat, sweater, phone, etc., vary the routine. Pick up the phone, put on a sweater and grab the keys, then put them back and sit down. Keep changing things up without leaving.
3. Repeat steps 1 and 2 until the dog is calm and nonreactive to the new routine.
4. After Phase 1 has been mastered and step 3 completed, add sending the dog to a quiet spot like her bed/crate or containment area. If GO FIND IT is a familiar command, tweak it to: GO TO YOUR BED.

Note: The time it takes to change a dog's association to departure triggers will vary among dogs.

Sophie became less reactive and calmer after practicing multiple repetitions of desensitization to my departure cues. The next step involved a command that would let her know that, when I left, she had a task. Dogs that have a workaholic canine-ality respond well to occupational commands. Sophie already knew GO FIND IT, so she easily adapted to GO TO YOUR BED. To be sure that she had plenty to do, I filled a Kong with yummy treats as well as left her some chew bones and toys. My heading out the door became a new routine for her wherein she perceived my departure as a task (GO TO YOUR BED) and a reward (Kong filled with yummy treats).

Note: Desensitizing Sophie to my departure cues took less than six weeks with four or five daily repetitions during which I consistently spot-checked her behavior using the web camera.

SEVERE SEPARATION ANXIETY

For owners whose dogs suffer from extreme canine separation anxiety, review the types of anxious behaviors listed earlier in the chapter. Additionally you might find:

- Exits and entrances with claw marks, chew marks or general destruction (the dog's attempts to get to you).
- Window areas marked with sweaty paw marks, or scratch marks on sills.
- Self-mutilation (chewing, licking at paws).
- A dog digging in an attempt to tunnel out of a fenced-in yard or engaging in destructive chewing on the wire mesh or wood boards of the fence.
- Urination and/or defecation.

Note: Separation anxiety may not always be the cause of destructive or acting-out behavior. Many dogs engage in those behaviors because they are bored, are not getting enough exercise or are under-socialized. In other cases of extreme separation anxiety, medication, in tandem with training, may be necessary.

Reminders for severe separation anxiety:

- Contact an experienced professional trainer to implement more specific treatment.
- Seek out a trainer who is skilled in positive reinforcement methods and familiar with desensitization and counterconditioning techniques.
- Get a medical checkup that includes testing for thyroid issues, impacted anal glands, or bladder, ear, tooth and urinary tract infections.

Other practical remedies for separation anxiety:

- Dietary changes
- Exercise
- Socialization
- Dog Appeasing Pheromone—D.A.P. collars and diffusers
- Doggy day care
- Crate training (p. 114)
- Body wraps (Thundershirt)
- Calming flower essences (chicory, heather, Rescue Remedy, etc.)
- Tellington Touch massage
- Interactive toys (Kong, Busy Buddy toys, bully sticks, Flossies, Nina Ottosson board games)

Sophie exemplifies how a dog responds to stress, anxiety and fear in a unique way. Anxious dogs are complex animals that need special care and training. These particular dogs are smart, sensitive and often under-stimulated. They teach us so much about dogs and our relationship with them and ourselves. My own dog, Sophie, was a challenge. Her low-level separation anxiety came at an inopportune time for me. Yet maybe because of it, I became a better trainer.

The chart below briefly summarizes how cooperation training and a behavior modification plan dovetail to fulfill a dog's specific needs as well as manage his particular anxiety (in this case, Sophie's).

Sophie's Issue	Cooperation Training and Behavior Management Approach
Strong pack drive (low-level separation anxiety)	Reinforcing Professor Sophie's pack drive through her role of teaching canine 101 manners to pups manages her anxiety (being with me) and gets her to focus more on the task at hand, not on me (expanding her threshold).
	Using her workaholic canine-ality to my training advantage was the perfect way to lower her pack drive needs.
	Ignoring unwanted "tantrum" behavior conditioned her to make the association that restrained, calmer behavior earns my attention.
	Implementing "exercise, exercise, exercise and socialize" exhausted her mentally and physically. Now when I take a shower or am getting ready to step out for an evening with friends, her expression says, *"I'm so tired. Please just tell me to GO TO MY BED."*
	Providing her with a food-filled Kong or chew toy appeased her workaholic canine-ality while serving as a "task" (and sometimes her dinner).

Sophie's Issue	Cooperation Training and Behavior Management Approach
Free-floating anxiety expressed by spinning	Applying SIT, DOWN and DOWN-STAY commands (counterconditioning) refocused her behavior.
	Stimulating her mind and increasing physical exercise using commands (GO FIND IT and FETCH).
	Upping the training ante placed SPIN activity on a cue, not her whim. This allowed me to control her spin impulse.

GET ON BOARD!

If you have an extremely anxious dog, it's always advisable to seek out professional help. Though I've acquired years of field experience and learned to read canine body language and respond to its subtleties, I'm not a licensed medical practitioner. Owners hire me for obedience and behavioral training. If a medical condition is causing the problem, or anti-anxiety prescription medicines are needed, then a veterinary behaviorist must be engaged. Behavior-modifying drugs for dogs significantly impacted by fear and anxiety can help improve a dog's and an owner's quality of life.

I often consult with E'Lise Christensen, DVM, a board-certified veterinary behaviorist in New York City. When considering the use of prescription medicine, some things Dr. Christensen keeps in mind are:

- The medical health of the animal.
- The desperation of the owner to solve the problem.
- The willingness of the owner to adhere to a prescribed behavior modification plan and to follow through with the treatment.
- The dog's level of suffering.

If a behavior modification plan is not in place, the anxious and fearful dog's and owner's lives can become agonizing and heartbreaking. The purebred with aggressive behavior that has earned shouts of "Control your dog!" on the street, or the sweet, once-housebroken Labradoodle who has become a bundle of nerves are both anxious dogs capable of plenty of good behavior. When not stressed or fearful, they'll quietly bring over toys for you to play with them. If you weren't clear on the *"Play with me"* hints, they'll nose-nudge you and bring over yet another toy. With patience and a specific behavior modification plan, these dogs can become the dogs they were always meant to be, ones that can romp, roam and fetch with a sense of ease, balance and good behavior.

Health: Mind, Body and Wag

Canine health starts with a well-balanced diet, exercise, playtime and sufficient sleep. Annual checkups should be part of the routine, along with regular grooming and plenty of tailgating. If you are aware of a specific ailment, proper veterinary care is important. However, changes in behavior can signify something is amiss.

A dog's only means of communicating his physical, emotional and health needs is through behavior. Regressive, lethargic, anxious, aggressive, disoriented and even obsessive behavior are often mistaken for "poor" behavior. But each can be an indication of a distressing health condition requiring immediate medical care.

The following chart provides examples of behaviors that in my experience can be linked to possible medical conditions.

Behavior	Possible Medical Condition
Regression in housebreaking	Urinary or bladder infection
Lethargy, sluggishness or weight gain	Hypothyroidism—(check thyroid)
Anxious or aggressive behavior (excessive shedding can be a physical symptom)	Hypothyroidism—(check thyroid)
Disorientation, distraction, confusion, irritability	Canine Cognitive Dysfunction (age-related senior dementia), impaired vision or hearing, diabetes or hypothyroidism
Obsessive licking of paws or scratching	Allergies, Canine Cognitive Dysfunction (age-related senior dementia)
Scooting, restlessness, general discomfort	Impacted anal glands or anal glands needing to be expressed
Loss of appetite, withdrawn, irritable	Periodontal disease or tooth or gum infection

Note: This chart provides owners with insight but should not be viewed or used as prescriptive diagnosis. My field of expertise is not in veterinarian medicine, but in canine obedience and behavioral training.

A dog's health care is an owner's lifelong responsibility. It involves comprehensive preventive care and seeks timely medical attention for injuries and illnesses.

SENSITIVE TO TOUCH

To treat a congenital defect, Paco underwent surgery on one of his front and back legs. He was just six months old when steel plates and numer-

Paco's behavior was being impacted by congenital defects, a low thyroid condition and the onset of arthritis.

ous screws were inserted into leg joints. "The first time we picked him up in the hospital, the staff said he'd been a fantastic patient," said Annie, Paco's owner. "I took him home and he whimpered the whole time. When I asked about his reaction, they said, 'He's probably telling you what a bad time he had.' The second time he whimpered less. He's such a good boy."

Paco was rescued with Casey, his littermate, a nine-week-old Labrador–pit bull mix. Both are pack-driven dogs with low fight drives. Casey is a party girl to the core. Paco is the methodical thinker with a sensitive soul. His personality resembles that of a kid content to read a book in the middle of a birthday party. He likes being in the room with all the shenanigans, but would never be the type to put a lamp shade on his head and dance on the table. He simply wants to take it all in, and he'll find the best seat in the house for viewing the action. Call him a spectator player.

"Paco had the most beautiful little face. He looked so sorry for himself," said Annie. "He was also the runt of the litter. I have a soft spot for things like that. He's a very loyal friend, but unlike Casey, at first he wouldn't come to you for affection. We honored his boundaries and waited for him to gain comfort in coming to us. Every dog has a sweet spot, the place they love to be petted. His is located just at the top of his tail. Give him a rub there and he loves it, but elsewhere he is still sensitive to being touched. It wasn't until I started working with Kate that I became aware that his surgeries were the underlying cause of his sensitivity to being touched."

ANNUAL HEALTH CHECK

It's important to take charge of your dog's health, including diet, exercise, mental stimulation, grooming and socialization. A veterinary health check should always be scheduled to rule out any underlying medical condition that may be altering a dog's daily activities. For dogs over eight years of age, I recommend a biannual health check.

Annual Health Check Includes:

- Weight and body condition
- TPR (temperature, pulse, respiration)
- Ophthalmoscopic exam of eyes
- Scope visualization of ears
- Reflexes, gait (checking a dog's movement)
- Attitude and activity level
- Examination of coat, nails, skin and anal glands
- Ensuring vaccinations are up-to-date
- Blood screening (thyroid, heartworm, liver and kidney diseases)
- Fecal examination (hookworm, roundworm, whipworm, coccidium and giardia)

Note: Consider a vaccine titer test if you feel your pet has adequate immunological protection from previous vaccines. This test can measure antibody levels in blood and properly assess the immune system's response.

SELECTING A VETERINARIAN

Choosing the right vet for you and your dog is important. You want someone who is current with medical advancements. I like vets who are also open-minded to alternative and holistic treatments such as acupuncture. Talk to other dog owners to get vet recommendations and visit a potential clinic prior to making an appointment.

After you have your first appointment, ask yourself:

- Was the facility clean?
- Was the exam thorough?
- Was the experience comfortable for my dog and myself?
- Did the doctor give my dog the proper attention?
- Did he/she handle my dog gently or was he/she too forceful?
- Did he/she take enough time to explain things and answer questions?
- Were the fees comparable to other vets in the area?

The following chart provides recommended Do's and Don'ts for forming a partnership with a veterinarian.

Do's	Don'ts
DO make sure your vet is receptive to questions, such as: Can he/she recommend a trainer? Does he/she have, or can he/she recommend, a twenty-four-hour clinic? Should the dog be microchipped or tattooed for ID purposes?	DON'T be afraid to ask questions and to do your own research. Consider: Would you recommend getting a second opinion? Is there a generic brand available? Is there a more cost-effective procedure that will not compromise my dog's health?
DO respect the vet's time. Prepare your questions in advance and write them down so you don't forget them.	DON'T treat the staff with less respect than the vet. Value them as an additional resource.
DO ask about medicine or vaccine side effects and potential problem signs you should look for.	DON'T call at peak hours with non-emergency questions. E-mail or wait until the end of the day.
DO make sure your vet is conscientious with follow-up care.	DON'T hold a veterinarian to a different standard of care than you would a physician for yourself or other members of your family.
DO find out about the tests they want to run on your dog.	DON'T be afraid to ask a vet to explain a procedure he/she would like to perform and if there are side effects or potential physical implications.

ADAPTABLE AND RESILIENT

Dogs are remarkably adaptable and resilient when it comes to health challenges. They have no problem telling us someone is at the front door or nose-nudging or play bowing when they want attention or are bored. Dogs will bark, bring us their leashes or coax using expressive raised eyebrows with a slight cock of the head that induces guilt when they want us to take them to the park. But they're not necessarily good at letting us know about health issues. Telling us when they're sick, in pain or off their game can be more of a challenge. To protect themselves from predators, their inherent survival instincts are geared toward concealing any signs of illness.

Paco bounced back after his two surgeries, although he was still sensitive to touch. His activity level demonstrated the typical behavior of a healthy dog. His strong pack drive and loyalty to his owners made training a rewarding and cooperative process. The commands were hands-free, honoring Paco's threshold of tolerance. His reactivity to squirrels, skateboards and excitement barking were managed and counterconditioned with LOOK-AT-ME, STAY, LEAVE IT and GO-TO-YOUR-CRATE commands.

HEALTH FROM HEAD TO TAIL

Many dogs ignore commands, but some have legitimate reasons. Deafness can come on suddenly, or gradually with age. The same is true of vision loss. If Boomer is banging into the furniture, it's unlikely he stopped by the dog run for a quick martini. Be proactive with a dog's health and examine him from head to tail. This includes looking at his poop.

Fecal size depends on the breed, but a firm, moist consistency is considered desirable. Hard stool can cause a dog to strain too much while eliminating. It may be a sign that he's not getting enough water, or it could be linked to a dietary or other health-related issue. Be on the lookout for blood, unusual mucus or rice-shaped particles, which might be worms. With diarrhea, the concern is related to frequency and duration.

The same is true with vomiting. Avoiding dehydration is of utmost importance.

If you suspect your dog isn't feeling well, take his temperature with a digital rectal thermometer. Placing a small dab of petroleum jelly on the bulb of the thermometer will make the insertion (an inch or less depending on the size of the dog) more comfortable. Hold it in position for about three seconds, then gently remove it. Normal temperature range is 101 to 102.5 degrees. Temperatures 99 degrees or lower or above 102.5 should be closely monitored and indicate that an owner should contact their veterinarian.

GROOMING

To maintain health, dogs need proper grooming. Be sure to focus on the following:

Body Part	Recommended Care
Eyes	Wipe gently around the eye, starting at the inner corner. Use a dampened cotton ball and remove eye gunk. Clean daily.
Ears	Dampen a cotton ball with hydrogen peroxide or an ear cleaner. Gently wipe the interior of the ear. Avoid sticking your finger in the ear canal and never use a cotton swab. Healthy ears are free of odor. An odor or a dark substance (not wax) could indicate a yeast infection. Check with a vet. Clean daily.
Nails	Regular clipping prevents nails from snagging or curling under. Curling can cause pain and even hamper a dog's ability to walk.

Body Part	Recommended Care
	Clip as needed (by owner, vet or vet tech). Be careful not to cut the quick, i.e., the soft inner part that protects blood vessels and nerves.
Teeth	Special toothbrushes, toothpaste and rinses are available for canine dental care. For small breeds, try a plastic finger toothbrush, which can be found in the baby section of drugstores.
	Real bones and Flossies are helpful to maintain teeth.
	Excessive bad breath can be an indication of periodontal disease.
	Check for broken or loose teeth.
	Clean daily (ideal) or twice weekly (minimum)
Coat/skin	Regular brushing keeps a coat shiny and avoids dirt buildup and matting.
	Long-haired dogs may require clipping and more frequent bathing.
	Check the skin for hot spots, bald patches, discolorations, bumps and cysts.
	Dogs, like people, can suffer from dermatitis related to allergies that are airborne or food- or environmentally related.
	Brush as needed.
Skin Folds	Certain breeds, like pugs, bulldogs, bloodhounds and Pekingese, have folds on their bodies where skin rubs together. Facial folds on these dogs are very common and can easily become inflamed and infected. Topical or oral antibiotics may be necessary.
	Check daily and clean as needed.
Nose	Doesn't need to be cleaned but check for cracking, scabs or sores. Discharge could be an indication of a sinus infection or kennel cough.

MONTHLY ROUTINE MAINTENANCE

Heartworm: Large worms that live in the heart of a dog. They're found in other animals, but dogs are the common host for this parasite. Heartworm is transmitted by the bite of an infected mosquito. It's a very dangerous disease that can kill a dog. It's preventable with a dose of a monthly easy-to-take tablet. Some veterinarian-recommended heartworm-preventive products are Heartgard Plus and Interceptor.

Fleas and Ticks: There are plenty of options to protect a dog from a wide range of medical challenges presented by fleas and ticks (e.g., Lyme disease, Rocky Mountain spotted fever and dermatitis). Whenever a dog comes in from outdoors, check his body, eyes, ears and mouth area for ticks. Some veterinarian-recommended flea-and-tick-preventive products are Frontline and Advantage. Also ask your doctor for holistic remedies.

JUST NOT HIMSELF

On a rainy day, an arthritic dog will likely become more sensitive and reactive to being touched or handled. Another pooch may seem distracted, or not interested in his food. This might be attributed to having a toothache or an ear or viral infection. Sluggish, lethargic and irritable responses could indicate a number of conditions. A dog's divergent behavioral changes are expressive communication signals that owners shouldn't ignore.

Owners often sense when a dog just isn't himself. This is what I call being the Sherlock Canine Holmes for your dog. Look for signs and don't ignore your owner instincts when it comes to knowing your dog. Some dogs can be asymptomatic and will need to count on your intuitive care. One owner told me that her dog doesn't scoot or exhibit typical behavior when his anal glands need expressing: "I know it's time because he takes on a Woody Allen, frenetic-like behavior."

IT'S ALL IN THE DETAILS

When a dog exhibits signs he's ill or his behavior is off, it helps if owners write down his training and medical and lifestyle details. On paper the details help an owner, trainer or veterinarian make a proper evaluation about your dog's health.

Below is a chart of Paco's training, medical and lifestyle details.

Paco's Training, Medical and Lifestyle Details

- Paco's owners have been conscientious from day one. As puppies, both dogs were socialized and exposed to many different people, objects and circumstances.
- Paco underwent two surgeries at six months of age for congenital defects on his front and back legs. Another operation was completed on his other back leg a few years later.
- Paco and Casey completed basic obedience training with another trainer.
- Owners hired me when Paco was one and a half years old. They wanted a more personalized training approach. We started right away with the Canine Drive Survey and determined each of their canine-alities.

- Since puppyhood, a neighborhood dog consistently lunged and barked at Paco. For three years, Paco ignored the dog, looked away and was nonreactive. Then one day the canine hoodlum started up with his bullying tactics and Paco barked back. Without additional reactivity, he turned back to his owners and kept walking. Paco's *"Knock it off"* bark demonstrated patience, not aggression.
- When owners were expecting their first child, both dogs, at three years of age, successfully completed my Baby on the Way program. Baby on the Way targets canine preemptive desensitization to all things "baby"-related. The ideal time to start sessions is around the mother's third month of pregnancy.

FAST-FORWARD PACO (AGE SIX)

Paco treasures the family and always picks the middle of wherever the children are playing for his destination spot to lie down. He chooses to be in the center of things and he takes it all in with great pride and pleasure. The following incidents happened that made his owners reevaluate his behavior:

- A visiting friend decided to show the children how to train a dog to sit. His tone was forceful and he pushed down the dog's bottom. The owners politely intervened, but it was beyond Paco's threshold of tolerance. He reacted by mouthing the friend on his arm without breaking the skin. It served to warn, not hurt, this person. The reaction, though provoked, was not acceptable to the owners.
- During the same time frame, their son was roughhousing with Paco. Again he reacted, though less so than before. There was no broken skin or bruising.

During both interactions, Paco tried to get away but was unsuccessful. The owners were seconds short of intervening and saw both incidents from an objective viewpoint. They understood Paco's response, but still found it unacceptable, even though no one was hurt. Despite having been pushed beyond his threshold of tolerance, mouthing is not an acceptable behavior.

His owners contacted me right away to address this issue. The first thing I recommended was a health check. At any age, a dog can have an underlying medical condition that impacts his behavior. I suggested a thyroid test and X-rays. Canine thyroid issues can be a source of increased reactivity and irritability. To err on the side of caution, they had also taken him to a veterinarian behaviorist for evaluation. It's also important to note that, prior to the two incidents, Paco had undergone a third surgery on his back leg.

Paco's previous behavioral history didn't indicate aggression. His mouthing had been controlled and used to warn, not hurt, anyone. New house rules were implemented to ensure Paco was not being provoked. The children, supervised at all times, were reminded to honor and be respectful of his boundaries. Playing with him was still encouraged, but by using "let him come to you" or "toss a toy to him and tell him to FETCH," the owners wanted the children to realize he was still playful but in a different way from Casey. Paco showed his affection by hanging out with them and following them from room to room. The kids began to see him as the "quiet buddy" who adored them.

The Results Are In

Paco's blood work showed a low thyroid condition and the physical exam indicated the onset of arthritis. This was a good time to think about the following:

- Why has Paco been wary of being touched since puppyhood?
- Has he been in pain since birth?
- Has his coping mechanism of "avoiding touch" been strategic and to reduce pain?

Paco's Medical Notes

- Veterinarian behaviorist assessment of Paco finds him to be a well-adjusted, nonaggressive dog.
- The veterinarian prescribes thyroid medication that stabilizes his mood and energy, helping to modify his behavior.

Paco's Dislikes	Triggered Behavior	Health Issue
Being touched in certain areas.	Keeping a comfortable distance (avoidance behavior).	Chronic pain due to genetics, arthritis and post-trauma from surgical procedures.
Being dominated, forced into a position, and roughhoused with.	Trying to get away (flight drive) and then reacting defensively by mouthing (fight drive).	Same as above. Bullying by others aggravated him, impacting his mental welfare.

TRAINING TECHNIQUES SPECIFIC TO PACO

Paco is a sensitive soul, not a reactionary dog, though at six he seems to be becoming less tolerant due to increased pain from arthritis. His low thyroid level problem, which is being treated, is likely compounding his present and potential future behavioral issues. The solution is to be respectful of his boundaries and limitations. His training techniques have changed. SIT is now a DOWN-STAY for him. This was done to reduce pressure on his joints and place him in a more comfortable position for longer periods of time. Canine hydrotherapy, an underwater treadmill, has been suggested in order to maintain a weightless, strenuous exercise routine.

Bite Inhibition Training: Paco has always been known to have a gentle mouth. Paco's owners: "When you give him a treat and say, 'Gentle,' he responds in a delicate manner. It's the same with his toys."

Paco's mouth control is exceptional. That being the case, we decided to advance his training by working with a dumbbell. Paco was taught to "TAKE IT" (pick up dumbbell) and then to "DROP IT" for ten to twenty repetitions, twice a day. Creating predictable and reliable behavior was the goal that then gave the owner another level of control. If placed in a challenging situation, such as the previous incident, DROP IT would easily translate into "NO" and place a behavioral safety brake in place.

FEATURED TRAINING TECHNIQUE: DROP IT

<table>
<tr><td>

Quick Description: DROP IT

DROP IT is a release command.

Teaching this command to dogs that are overly protective of their toys or bones (resource guarding) is useful.

It's also a play mandate required for making FETCH an enjoyable and partnered activity.

GOAL: to establish cooperative behavior so that a dog willingly releases and drops on cue.
</td></tr>
</table>

DROP IT Steps

1. Offer your dog a chew bone or toy that he really loves and encourage him to take it in his mouth while you hold on to the item. Have a yummy treat in the fist of your other hand.

2. When he takes the chew item in his mouth, place the fist with the treat next to his nose and mouth. He'll be able to smell the treat and he should instinctively release the bone or toy from his mouth. At that "release" moment, mark "YES" and praise as he eats the treat.

3. Offer the bone or toy again and repeat steps 1 and 2 five to ten times in different body stances (kneeling, lying down, standing). The goal is to get him to willingly release the item when he sees your fist.

4. Once he's reliably releasing the item, advance to adding the verbal cue. When he takes the offered item in his mouth, cue "DROP IT." As he relinquishes the item, immediately mark it and give him a JACKPOT REWARD (p. 21) and praise. Repeat five to ten times.

5. Progress to delaying the reward. Cue "DROP IT," but this time as

the dog releases the item, praise him and reveal an empty hand without treats. Wait three seconds and then treat. The aim is to establish a responsive "DROP IT" without relying on a treat.

6. Practice "DROP IT" with a variety of items (old slipper, sock, outdated remote, dishrag) to ensure "DROP IT" translates to everything. "DROP IT" repetitions need to be trained in different locations to ensure that it means anytime and anywhere.

Note: Be playful with all commands since learning is best accomplished in a relaxed and pleasurable atmosphere.

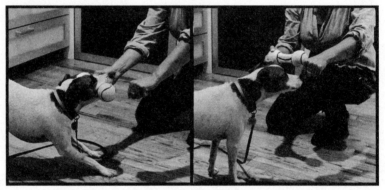

Teaching Tucker the DROP IT command managed and trained his bite inhibition and advanced into interactive playtime with his owners.

Paco's owners: "I now give him thyroid medication twice a day by pushing the tablets into his mouth. He never tries to bite down. He's simply sweet about it. We also keep an eye on his diet with a careful emphasis on keeping his weight at fifty-five pounds. Maintaining a lower weight is another way to ease the pressure on his joints."

DIET

A dog's diet can arguably be considered the most influential aspect of canine health and behavioral issues. Yet knowing how to pick a dog's food can be challenging. Choosing the right food will directly impact how your dog feels, acts and functions. Is protein revving up your dog? Or is a lack of sufficient protein the cause of lethargic behavior, a dull coat or even irritability? Grains (i.e., corn and wheat) may cause allergic reactions in some pooches while others can tolerate them without a problem.

DESIGNER LABELS

Pet food quality is a confusing and controversial topic. Reading labels can be daunting. A Statement of Nutritional Adequacy is required by law and generally can be found near the wording "Association of American Feed Control" or "AAFCO," which is a voluntary organization that regulates and uniformly labels pet food.

The Statement of Nutritional Adequacy lists the following on the labels:

Statement of Nutritional Adequacy	Translated to Mean:
"Complete and balanced nutrition"	Meets all dog nutritional requirements.
"Growth" or "for all life stages"	Suitable for dogs and puppies.
"Maintenance"	Suitable for adult dogs.

Something else to consider when reading labels is that ingredients must be listed according to weight. Greater amounts are listed first. Look for products that list "chicken," "lamb," "beef," "duck" or "salmon" first. If the word "meal" follows chicken, lamb or beef, it means these ingredients have been dried and ground up into a formula that includes bones. Not something you'd serve at the dinner table.

"By-products" are common ingredients found in most dog food. They can include organ meat, intestines and other undesirable ingredients. This is an inexpensive way for pet food companies to keep protein levels listed as "high" while not being high quality. Excluded from "by-products" listings are hair, horns, teeth and hooves.

Grains, too, are listed on labels. They may sound healthy, but are not necessarily biologically appropriate for dogs. In a canine body, grains don't metabolize the same way they do in ours. This can result in an accumulation of lactic acid, which can cause muscular pain and allergies. Since grains are full of carbohydrates, which are easily converted to sugar, there may be a link between them and cancer in cats and dogs since cancer cells feed off of sugar. The grains used are also often those that are unfit for human consumption because they contain mold and other contaminants.

The list goes on, so I urge you to become Sherlock Canine Holmes, not only with training, but also with diet. Go online, investigate and understand what you are really feeding your dog.

A dog should never have alcohol, chocolate or coffee. Depending on the amount consumed, all three can impact the central nervous system and be toxic and possibly fatal for your dog. Take the time to become familiar with other items, listed below, that also should be avoided.

Ingredients to Avoid Giving a Dog

- Alcohol
- Avocado
- Any candy containing the sweetener Xylitol
- Beverages with caffeine (soda, tea, coffee)

- Bread dough
- Cat food (Cat food is not formulated for canine consumption. It is generally too high in protein and fat and not balanced for a dog.)
- Chocolate
- Cooked bones (Cooked bones can be very hazardous to your dog. Bones become brittle when cooked, causing them to splinter when chewed and creating a choking hazard. Raw bones, like chicken necks or beef knucklebones, are generally considered safe and help keep your dog's teeth healthy by removing plaque.)
- Corncobs (Corncobs can cause a partial or complete intestinal obstruction.)
- Dairy products for lactose intolerant dogs.
- Fatty foods (Rich, fatty foods can be very dangerous for dogs susceptible to attacks of pancreatitis.)
- Fruit pits (Apple, peach, apricot, cherry, pear, plum and other pits from fruit can cause cyanide poisoning.)
- Garlic (raw, cooked or powdered)
- Grapes and raisins
- Macadamia nuts and walnuts
- Moldy foods
- Mushrooms
- Mustard seed
- Onions and onion powder

EXERCISE

Losing weight and getting in shape physically and mentally are the primary reasons people exercise. The same principles hold true for dogs. The benefits of canine workouts, just like the benefits of human workouts, go far beyond weight loss. Exercise is preventative care for:

- Cardiac disease
- Osteoarthritis
- Compromised immune functions
- Respiratory problems
- Cognitive dysfunction
- Ligament injuries

Coupled with a balanced diet, exercise increases serotonin and endorphin levels, which produces a calm, relaxed and happy dog. In high concentrations, these neurochemicals are known to reduce anxiety, relieve depression, enhance pleasure and suppress pain—emotional and physical. They're natural and can easily be acquired through physical and mental activities.

Physical

- Walking
- Fetching
- Playing Frisbee
- Obedience training
- Hiking
- Jogging
- Swimming
- Herding competitions
- Freestyle play (canine dancing)
- Agility training (professional and at home)
- Rally competitions (combining obedience and agility)
- Visiting dog parks
- Going to doggy day care
- Having playdates

Mental

- Activity toys
- Interactive food dispenser
- Treasure hunt (owner-crafted—e.g., can be as simple as a draw-string fabric bag stuffed with toys)
- Tidying tasks (owner-crafted—e.g., "Put away your toys")

Exercise is also a bond-building activity. SIT, DOWN, STAY and COME are commands as well as exercises. There are at least five "exercise-training" opportunities built into our daily lives: three walks a day and two feeding times. These can be used to practice and master obedience commands while simultaneously giving the dog stimulating physical and mental workouts.

Below is Professor Sophie's daily "exercise-training" opportunities chart that can easily be adapted to fit into most any owner's lifestyle.

Requirements	Exercise-Training Opportunities
Morning relief walk	LOOK-AT-ME and TOUCH TARGET (5–10 repetitions)
Breakfast	DOGGY PUSH-UPS, also known as SIT-DOWN repetitions
Afternoon relief walk	LEAVE IT (cooperation and focus drills) and SPIN (crowd-pleasing trick that burns off excess energy)
Dinner	GO FIND IT (mental and physical workout) Turns on her scavenger instinct and lets her earn his meal.
Evening relief walk	Stop by the dog run, let her interact with other dogs (tailgating) and practice COME when it's time to go home.

ECONOMICS OF A CANINE-PAIRED EXERCISE BUDDY

Owners on a budget can save money and still keep in great shape while strengthening the bond with their dog. Rethink the gym membership because Fido can replace a personal trainer. Your dog can satisfy the reasons you'd hire a personal trainer. He'll provide you with motivation, an individualized program and efficiency.

- **Motivation:** Dogs are around-the-clock movers and shakers. They get you out and about in the world. Of course there are plenty of couch potato pooches, but most will walk over to you with their leash in their mouth in a ready-to-go formation.
- **Individualized Program:** Cooperation dog training specifically targets a dog's unique needs and an owner's lifestyle.
- **Efficiency:** There's no need to run to the gym or put on stretch or sweat-resistant clothing. Wear what you like, leash up and bring along a thermos filled with coffee or tea.

Besides being cost-effective, exercise training is a great way to spend time with your dog. It also replaces being confined to an indoor gym. Explore the streets the same joyous way Rover does. Whether in a city, suburb or rural environment, there's always something new to discover on every walk. Exercise is a physical and mental must-do daily activity.

PLAYTIME

Play perfectly balances training, exercise, mental stimulation and bonding. It also ensures social needs at both ends of the leash are being met.

The interaction between owners and dogs, and dogs and other dogs, is so important that the last chapter is devoted entirely to play. Play encourages proper behavior and aids in the development of motor and social skills. It can also be used to train essentials such as bite inhibition. Play is seriously a fun part of training. I'll talk more about it in chapter 12.

REST

Getting enough rest applies to all species, not just humans. During rest periods, the immune system optimizes and allows for the proper functioning of organs. Lack of sleep can cause irritability, especially for a dog that may already be operating off a fight-or-flight drive. Puppies in particular need downtime for their developing bodies. A sign that the canine workouts are achieving their desired goals is seeing your pooch curled up comfortably on the floor next to you.

HEALTH: MIND, BODY AND WAG CONCLUSION

Common sense and preventive care is always advised when it comes to canine health. Dogs can't take themselves to a veterinarian and delays could exacerbate a problem. Health checks can often reveal an underlying cause for unwanted behavior. Remember that a behavior can be linked to health, diet, genetics or environment. A dog's health is dependent on an owner making good decisions for him. A proper amount of physical and mental stimulation is the key to successful canine guardianship. Though a veterinarian administers medical care, a dog's health is ultimately the owner's responsibility.

Leash Lingo

f you reached this chapter then your training résumé includes the following:

- A familiarity with training concepts and terms.
- Reliability with go-to Pay Attention commands LOOK-AT-ME and TOUCH TARGET.
- An understanding of the canine drives: pack, prey, flight and fight.
- The ability to match up and make distinctions between canine-ality and personality.
- Puppyhood and housebreaking fundamentals.
- Ten commands and several instructional how-to sections that include crate training.
- Tailgating event planning.
- A working knowledge of desensitizing and counterconditioning canine anxiety.

- An understanding that a behavior issue can stem from an underlying medical condition.

Putting it all together, leashing it up and taking it on the road is the next step. The outdoor walk is the time many owners prepare to go into battle. Grabbing a leash, securing it to a collar and stepping outside comes with trepidation and concern. The vicious cycle of leash reactivity, often unknowingly reinforced by an owner, kicks into high gear at the sight of another dog, person or circumstance. It's a common behavior challenge for many dogs no matter what the breed or background. A purebred, mixed breed or rescue dog can be well mannered indoors, but once outdoors and on-leash, display the near equivalent of road rage. The leisurely stroll turns into a nightmare.

Maybelline, a two-year-old re-homed stray with inch-long eyelashes, was a canine supermodel. This cocker spaniel was highly reactive on-leash and inclined to lunge out of control. She'd be positioned on her two hind legs for blocks at a time responding to passing dogs. Her rearing-stallion stance was wearing out her owner.

"It was so bad that when people or dogs wanted to meet my cutie, I'd pull her between parked cars and say, 'My girl's rowdy—please don't come over to us and say hello,'" said Toni, Maybelline's owner. "I dreaded my walks with her. She was an adversary, not a companion. People would cross the street to get

Maybelline's owner uses her leash not to dominate her dog but as a management tool to counter leash reactivity.

away from us. The moment I snapped the leash on her, my stomach would knot up. I really thought I could handle anything, but I was having serious doubts about Maybelline."

Preparing for a pleasurable loose-leash walking experience is in part about choosing the right equipment with the proper fit and being self-assured when giving commands. Gear and accessories, like canine drives, canine-alities and learning styles, also need to be customized to address the specific needs of a dog.

With so many products on the market, how do you decide what equipment to purchase for your dog? What factors do you need to consider? What about the fit? My equipment recommendations are specific. I want owners to work with the best training tools possible. An owner who calls me about a leash issue is frustrated. The relationship at both ends of the leash is strained. It doesn't have to be this way. Walking a dog should not be a battle.

Putting on the equipment is not necessarily intuitive. It also needs to be properly sized to fit in the way it was designed. Working with behaviorists and positive reinforcement trainers, manufacturers have researched and designed equipment to tackle pulling and reactive dogs—their criteria being an adjustable, ergonomic design producing a calming effect that allows for comfortable control aimed at simplifying training. When put on and sized properly, the equipment can change the leash dynamics. It's meant to encourage cooperation that tugs at your heart, not your shoulder socket! Leash challenges are real, but not impossible to fix.

CORD OF COMMUNICATION

Along with commands, the leash is an integral piece of equipment that transmits owner expectations to a dog. Failure to properly communicate can lead to reactivity.

Leash reactivity commonly stems from the following:

- Lack of training (unfamiliar with equipment)
- Socialization deficit (overwhelmed)
- Frustration (resisting being restrained)
- Excitement (limited impulse control)
- Boredom (pent-up energy)
- Aggression (feistiness or fear)

My training philosophy considers the leash a management tool, a guide crafted to give owners a way to understand the world from their dog's perspective. Owners working with these techniques are in a position of leading with managed control, not force.

Let the leash, recommended equipment and command training turn walking your dog into a pleasurable and relaxing stroll.

LEASH

- A leash is used to safely lead a dog, or hold him in check. It's an essential training and everyday management tool.
- Trainer recommendation: four-foot leash in leather or nylon. If you have a six-foot leash, tie three separate knots in it to shorten

the line. Use those knots as leash grips to vary the length. The grips help an owner rein in a reactive dog, or one in harm's way, without risking hand injury.

- Adjustable leads, which can be converted into short leashes for constrained walking areas, are coming onto the market. Some have a built-in traffic handle. The extreme jumping and lunging dog will benefit from early training with this lead, which easily becomes a temporary management tool to curb unwanted behavior.

Introducing a Leash to a Dog

1. Start indoors by offering high-value treats when clipping the leash onto the collar D-ring.
2. Once the leash is attached, let the dog drag it behind him to become acclimated to the feel of it while you supervise him. The goal is to build a *"no big deal"* attitude toward the leash.
3. If he starts to chew the leash, distract him with a toy. If he returns to chewing it, spray it with Grannick's Bitter Apple, a nontoxic chew deterrent.

Note: For larger and stronger breeds needing maximum control, consider a leash handle. This manages a dog by keeping him at your side and removes the need to wrap the leash around your hand to shorten it.

The following chart provides a brief overview of equipment that I recommend. Later in the chapter I provide steps on how to acclimate and fit equipment to your dog. Included are guidelines on choosing pieces targeted to a dog's behavior needs.

Equipment	Strengths and Trainer's Note on Equipment
Collar: Snap or buckle	**Strengths:** Easy to find and available in a variety of styles and colors. Backup security and good place to attach license and ID tags. **Trainer's Note:** Offers less control and, if restraint is necessary, possible choking or injury to neck, trachea or esophagus.
Head halters: Gentle Leader headcollar by Premier Pets (preferable for smaller breeds) Halti by the Company of Animals (preferable for larger breeds)	**Strengths:** Provides owners with greater steering power and control of the dog. Helps prevent jumping, lunging and excessive barking. It's not a muzzle and will not choke a dog. A dog can eat, drink and fetch while wearing it. **Trainer's Note:** Requires acclimation period. Accurate sizing is crucial to avoid it slipping off the dog. Problematic for short-nosed, limited-muzzle breeds. No-pull harnesses are a better option for brachycephalic breeds like pug, French bulldog and shih tzu.
No-pull harnesses: Sensation No-Pull Harness or Easy Walk Harness	**Strengths:** Greater control of a dog's movement without risk of choking or neck, trachea or esophagus injury. Good for dogs that pull or tug. **Trainer's Note:** Will not prevent jumping or lunging. A dog may resist walking until he becomes acclimated to the equipment.

Equipment	Strengths and Trainer's Note on Equipment
Martingale collar: A preferred padded collar	**Strengths:** Designed for dogs with narrow heads and sensitive necks, like greyhounds and whippets. Meant to prevent injuries (choking) and avoid any possibility of the dog slipping out of the collar. **Trainer's Note:** Less control over pulling, lunging and jumping.

SLED DOG

Maybelline was a classic under-socialized dog with no leash etiquette. Upon meeting and observing her, I guessed that she had been a backyard dog that had been left to roam. She had no training and likely no supervision. Perhaps a door was left ajar for a second and she wandered off.

"I'd bitten off more than I could chew with her," remarked Toni. For years her other dog, Buddy, had been sick and in need of constant medical attention. Toni took a part-time job to help pay for his care. "After dealing with Buddy and his illness, I thought I could handle anything, but I had no control over Maybelline. She was like a sled dog, pulling me every which way." Maybelline was also placing Toni and herself in potential danger.

A dog pulling, dragging and lunging on-leash is an accident waiting to happen. The interaction between dog and owner can often turn into a world-class tug-of-war. Typically owners unwittingly reinforce the very behavior (pulling, dragging, lunging) that they want eliminated. The dog with "leash excitement," as opposed to "leash aggression," can heed the wrong message from being jerked and yanked. Fido: *"Oooh, I get it, my owner's telling me this is a 'dangerous' dog or person. Silly me, I just wanted to say hello. Okay, game on* [barking]—'YOU WANT a PIECE OF ME—COME ON! I'M NOT AFRAID!'"

According to Hal Herzog, professor of psychology at Western Carolina University, over eighty-five thousand Americans are taken to emergency rooms each year because of falls caused by their pets.

ROLE REVERSAL

Asking an owner to reverse roles with a dog is a way for me to provide insight into a dog's on-leash behavior.

Leash Excitement: If you're walking down the street and see a friend up ahead, it's likely you'll pick up your pace to catch up with him.

Leash Frustration: If someone comes from behind, tugs you backward, then keeps you from meeting up with your friend, would it annoy you or make you feel anxious?

Leash Aggression: If a bicyclist cuts in front of you, would you react by being startled? Maybe angry?

The dog eager to greet another dog, or investigate a new territory or situation, can feel that the leash is restraining and holding him back. The tug-of-war stems from excitement and can quickly develop into leash frustration. Many trainers refer to the "yank-spank" dynamic as self-perpetuating at both ends of the leash. It's the catalyst that can advance leash frustration into leash aggression. The more a dog is pulled back, the more he becomes riled up and reflexively counter pulls.

Reactive leash issues are often complicated by not having the right equipment. Even with the right equipment, other issues such as under-socialization or lack of exercise can make it challenging to take a stroll.

The leash is tormenting to an under-socialized dog overwhelmed by being outdoors. It restrains and prevents him from being able to escape when frightened. Under-exercised dogs, or those stuck indoors all day because of inclement weather, have pent-up energy. They may become rambunctious and hard to handle when they finally go outside.

Excitement or Aggression

Being outdoors is an exhilarating social outlet for a dog. Excited and raring to go, he will seek companionship and interaction with other dogs. That's normal behavior. However, in my experience owner confusion often occurs because the reaction a dog has to leash excitement, or leash aggression, can appear as the same behavior. Both events display pulling, lunging, jumping and barking. The difference is a dog's intent. There's a "play and socialize" component to leash excitement, whereas "harm and fear" characterize leash aggression. Fido's on-leash excitement reactivity says, *"Gosh, that's Gator—gotta say hi and catch up with him."* Frustration develops if his socialization needs are not being met.

Preventing a dog from interacting with other dogs or people can also lead to behavior that's displayed as aggressive. The initial canine reaction, starting as excitement, develops into frustration, which can advance to on-leash aggression. A balanced approach that allows for normal dog interplay (with other dogs and people) is recommended. A sequestered dog is not living a quality life. Proper canine guardianship provides for all areas of a dog's welfare, including adequate shelter, suitable diet, care of physical and mental health and ample opportunity to exhibit normal behavior patterns. Managed control of a dog is important, but it shouldn't inhibit a dog from being a dog.

INDOOR MANNERS MATTER

My approach to desirable on-leash behavior starts indoors. Too often, leash issues overlook that Fido has been raised to habitually do as he pleases indoors. Effective canine guardianship starts with setting down ground rules at home. Running to the door every time the doorbell rings and barking madly or jumping on guests is unacceptable indoor canine behavior. If a dog is permitted to act this way indoors, why should he act differently outdoors? Training and managing indoor behavior is the best way to teach a dog what's expected of him outdoors.

Desirable "anytime and anywhere" canine behavior results when owners have properly addressed indoor issues. There's a harmony and co-ordination at both ends of the leash with expectations understood. Indoor training becomes the dress rehearsal that prepares both owner and dog for crowded sidewalks, hiking paths and the aisles of pet-friendly stores.

LOW IMPULSE CONTROL

For an owner not familiar with BASIC (Be Affirming Securing Impulse Control, p. 160) walking a dog with no impulse control can be an agonizing experience. This was the case for Toni and Maybelline. Putting on the leash and hitting the sidewalk can turn into a battle of wills. Why? Because the dog expects his "do as you please" demeanor, which was cultivated indoors, to be acceptable outdoors. A dog might also feel he has a job to do and a need to protect his owner. Either way, owners should take the leadership role and guide the dog so he knows how you want him to behave. Pulling the dog in an attempt to gain control fuels and reinforces his opposition reflex. He counters with tugging on the leash, which gives him the reward of moving him forward. Consequently, his heightened on-leash energy can lead to problematic behavior with public safety concerns. Stopping in your tracks and not pulling him is the best owner response.

Fido Type	Low-Impulse-Control Behavior
Street Mayhem Specialist (prey drive)	Leash reactivity set off by lunging, pulling or chasing a bicyclist, squirrel, skateboarder or baby stroller. The leash becomes a mere suggestion.
Fraidy Cat (flight drive)	Provoked by sirens, horns, thunder, dogs or blowing leaves. Further challenged because the leash makes escaping from a fearful situation difficult. The leash becomes a tormentor.
Mild-Mannered (pack drive indoors) to Rambo (fight drive outside)	The indoor pack-driven dog becomes protective on-leash. He takes on a "Rambo" persona, going paw-to-paw and jaw-to-jaw with anybody or any dog that dares to come near his pack members. The leash emboldens him.
Professional Puller and Dragger (pack, prey, flight and fight drives)	"Tug and drag" masters can weigh three to one hundred or more pounds. The featherweights often are the ones dominating their owners and taking home the "ON-LEASH WILL-OF-WAR CHAMPION" titles. Fido: *"Leash? What leash?"*

Even if a dog is not a threat to others, poor, laborious on-leash behavior wears an owner down and can tear apart the relationship. Low-impulse-control dogs often have fewer socializing opportunities because owners leave them at home to avoid the on-leash hassle. Owners of smaller dogs use pet carrier purses to avoid the chore-combative stroll. As a result, these dogs are more likely to become under-socialized and suffer from lack of exercise. In turn, their pent-up energy builds and ends up expressing itself through destructive or anxious behavior.

CUT SOME SLACK

When a dog is pulling, dragging or lunging on-leash, the owner's natural tendency is to pull or yank the dog back to his side. Resist that urge. Instead, come to a complete stop. The "yank-spank" teaches and reinforces a dog to continue pulling. It's called opposition reflex—a dog's ingrained instinct to push back against pressure. Change the pattern and teach him that when you stop, he should stop. Relax the leash; it's called loose-leash walking for a reason. Tension on a lead tells a dog to be on high alert. Owners need to cut their dogs some slack to avoid a tug-of-war.

GET YOUR LIFE BACK

Toni had been using a choke and prong collar on Maybelline. Expect the "OUCH" factor if the dog wearing a choke or prong collar makes one false move. From Maybelline's perspective, she was excited to meet other dogs. Her social etiquette lacked grace. She'd see a dog and lunge to greet them. Toni would pull her back, setting off Maybelline's opposition reflex. "Spotting a dog, she'd go ballistic," said Toni. A dog isn't versed in complex thinking. The association with a choke collar for a dog like Maybelline becomes: *"I see a dog and my neck gets squeezed by the choke collar. Then I feel pain. WOW! Those dogs are causing the pain. I don't like them. I better bark and lunge at them to go away so the pain stops."*

"The no-pull harness gave me back my life," said Toni.

I recommend this equipment because it's gentle yet effective for owner and dog when it comes to managing behavior.

Maybelline's Equipment	Specific Details
No-pull harness	Her choke collar was replaced with a no-pull harness.
Leash grip knots	Three leash grip knots were added to shorten Toni's six-foot lead. This increased the ability to keep Maybelline at a more manageable distance while making the leash more user-friendly.
Treat pouch	A treat pouch made the reinforcement training more convenient. It also served as a visual cue and scent aid for Maybelline's attention.

IT'S ALL IN THE DESIGN

I work with equipment that replicates the design elements of head halters used to safely and successfully manage twelve-hundred-pound horses. Sharing this information gets owners curious and interested in what else they don't know about the equipment.

Other design features of head halters and no-pull harnesses:

- They apply even pressure when a dog pulls the same way acupressure points do when you get a massage. If you get the right pressure on the back of your neck, it feels good and is calming.
- The head halter was fashioned to replicate the corrections of a mother dog disciplining her pups.
- Both pieces of equipment control and steer the head in a natural and safe way that works to guide, not force, a dog's movements.

What's complicated? The fit. When someone joins a gym and is surrounded by state-of-the-art equipment, a personal trainer may need to walk them through the mechanics and benefits of each machine. Think about the person who wants to build up his biceps but unwittingly works only his triceps because he's not using the equipment properly. It takes time to get accustomed to training equipment. It's not complicated—just unfamiliar to both you and your dog. Have patience. The right equipment will make walking with your dog pleasurable.

UNCOMPLICATING EQUIPMENT

Consulting a professional to review the basics—equipment needs, proper fit and an orientation on management tools—will alleviate frustration and save time for owners and dogs. Once the leash equipment has been properly fitted and used as designed, it functions as a management and training tool, establishing and supporting a welcoming loose-leash walk experience.

The following pages provide comprehensive detail about the equipment that I recommend.

COLLAR

- Choose a durable collar, leather or nylon, with a secure fastener (clasp or buckle). Attach the required dog license tag along with an engraved ID tag listing the dog's and owner's names, contact information, date of last rabies vaccination, microchip # and medical information (blind, deaf or diabetic; allergies).
- Tags can be taken off inside the home, but must always be worn outdoors or in unfamiliar settings.
- Remove collar and tags when a dog is alone, in the containment area or inside his crate.

Note: Consider embroidered ID collars for teacup breeds. They're lightweight and help avoid the jingle-jangle sound of tags. Alternatively, simply tape tags together.

Introduce a collar or harness to your dog just before feeding. This creates a positive association with the equipment. Fido: *"Collar on and food is served. Nice concept!"*

Reinforces	Counters
Pack drive: The ID collar signifies ownership and belonging.	Finders of lost dogs not knowing to whom they belong.

(Review leash and collar introduction on p. 88.)

Gentle Leader or Halti?

Both designs are similar to a bridle. They communicate to a dog through pressure on the muzzle and the back of the head instead of on the trachea and neck.

- Gentle Leader and Halti both require acclimation time. It's important to ensure the proper fit with a head halter. You guide the dog by steering him with his head slightly down and in a relaxed position.
- Gentle Leader is available in a wide assortment of colors for the style-conscious owner. Self-adhesive moleskin should be added to the inside of the Gentle Leader to prevent chafing around a dog's muzzle.
- Gentle Leader comes with fitting instructions, a training guide and a comprehensive training DVD.
- The Halti is softly lined to prevent skin irritation.
- The Halti has an extra clasp so a collar can be attached for added security.

Note: This is not a replacement for a basket muzzle. A head halter will not stop a dog from biting.

Introducing a Halti or Gentle Leader to a Dog

1. With a happy tone, show the dog the head halter and give him a high-value treat. Then hide the halter behind your back for ten seconds. Repeat this for five to ten repetitions until your dog is curious about the head halter.

2. Hold the muzzle part open and lure his nose through with a treat while praising him. Then hide the halter behind your back once again. Repeat this for five to ten repetitions. This should make him curious and interested in it.

3. Once the dog is voluntarily putting his nose through the halter and accepting it around his nose, loosely clip it at the base of his ears. It should rest on the top of his neck. Take two minutes to encourage him to chew on a bone or Kong, or engage him in any activity that he prizes as a distraction to help desensitize him to the equipment.

4. Take off the head halter and give the dog no attention.

5. Repeat steps 1 to 3. Once the dog accepts the head halter that you'll attach to a leash, practice walking around indoors (dress rehearsal). This will familiarize him with the feel of the head halter while walking. The leash attachment for head collars will not be used at this point.

6. Gradually tighten the muzzle strap (make sure one finger fits between the strap and the dog's muzzle) and continue walking the dog inside with a happy tone while tossing treats. Once you feel there's acceptance of the equipment, unclip the leash from the collar and attach it to the head halter D-ring. Use a JOLLY EFFECT voice and treats to motivate him to walk on-leash.

7. Once this is established indoors, take him outside for a walk. Be sure to work in the LOOK-AT-ME and TOUCH TARGET Pay Attention commands and lead with self-assured confidence.

Note: Expect him to shake his head and paw at the head collar. When this happens, be patient and use a happy tone to redirect his attention using commands (counterconditioning).

- Head halter (Gentle Leader or Halti)
- Buckle collar
- Tags
- Lead with built-in traffic handle
- Leash knot
- No-pull harness (SENSE-ation or Easy Walk)

Reinforces	Counters
Leadership: An owner is in control and guiding a dog's gaze and concentration.	Prey drive in dogs with propensity to scavenge. Fight drive, as dog is easily maneuvered away from another dog.

No-Pull Harness

- Front-Connection (SENSE-ation and SENSE-ible) and Easy Walk harnesses are designed to lead movement from a dog's chest, preventing him from pulling his owner. This equipment is for walking purposes only and should be taken off indoors. The chest straps are designed to rest EVENLY across the breastbone, thereby avoiding injury to the tracheal area.
- The Front-Connection (SENSE-ation and SENSE-ible) harness fits more securely across the chest of dogs with short legs and tiny elbows (French bulldogs, corgis, basset hounds) as well as mutts and designer breeds with unique body shapes.

Note: You should be able to attach the leash to the collar as well as the harness's front D-ring. This is especially important for dogs and owners in the early stages of training.

Introducing a No-Pull Harness to a Dog

1. Hold harness open and, using a high-value treat, lure the dog's nose through the harness.
2. Place some treats, or a filled Kong, on the ground to distract the dog and keep him busy while you clip the harness on. This creates a positive association with the equipment.
3. Snap on the clasp of girth strap underneath the left elbow of the dog. Then make the necessary adjustments to properly fit the size of your dog (one finger snug).
4. Adjust the shoulder straps to properly fit the dog (one finger snug).
5. Locate the dog's breastbone and adjust the chest straps so they're

equally proportioned and the D-ring is centered and lying flat across the chest.

6. Attach the leash to the D-ring.

Reinforces	Counters
Canine manners: An owner can easily redirect by pulling into a SIT or HEEL command, thereby controlling a dog's opposition reflex.	A dog's prey and fight drives by redirecting his movements. Pulling or dragging by maneuvering from the chest and girth, not the neck.

Martingale Collar

This collar was specifically designed for dogs with narrow heads and sensitive necks (saluki, Afghan hound, borzoi). It's also referred to as a limited-slip collar.

Introducing a Martingale Collar to a Dog

1. Using a high-value treat, lure the dog's head through the collar. (There are two loops: the smaller one is the control loop, where the D-ring is located; the second loop is used to tighten or loosen the collar.)

2. Slide the collar to the middle of the dog's neck and size as needed. Tighten so that you can fit two fingers snugly between the neck and the inside of the collar.

3. Attach the leash to the D-ring of the control loop. The control loop prevents the collar from slipping off the dog's head.

Reinforces	Counters
Responsible canine guardianship: The right equipment matters. Securing a dog comfortably and safely matters.	Houdini-like dogs adept at escaping the collar. When a dog tries backing out of the collar, it tightens without choking him.

WAG LINGUISTICS

Maybelline likely came from a puppy mill, not a reputable breeder, and she was left with a street challenge: a tail that had been docked to an extreme, leaving her virtually without one. A dog without a tail to wag is like someone texting while walking and in a hurry to get to work. He can do it, but it's a challenge, and certain words will be misspelled and expressions and tonality can easily be misinterpreted. Maybelline's floppy ears and long eyelashes that covered her eyes only added to the difficulty of reading her subtle expressions and body language.

Maybelline's "tail-less" communication disadvantage made it a challenge for Toni and other dogs to read her on-leash reactivity. Was Maybelline expressing excitement, frustration or aggression? The answer is that, at different times and in combination, all three behaviors were evoked. All dogs, depending on the context, will express excitement, frustration and aggression to varying degrees while on-leash. Establishing predictable loose-leash walk etiquette is about having the right equipment, reading your dog's responses to other dogs, people and circumstances, and using commands to redirect his attention when necessary.

It was more difficult for Toni to read if her dog was happy, concerned, alert, agitated or being aggressive. Redirecting Maybelline's behavior with LOOK-AT-ME and TOUCH TARGET commands while keeping a tension-free connection would be key to developing desirable loose-leash walking behavior.

FEATURED TRAINING TECHNIQUE: LOOSE-LEASH WALKING

Quick Description: Loose-Leash Walking

Loose-Leash Walking is when there's a tension-free connection that maintains the leash in an unrestricted L-shape.

Owner Anti-Pull Pledge: "If my dog pulls, without getting emotional, I'll come to a complete stop. I'll command 'LOOK-AT-ME' and TOUCH TARGET to redirect his focus into cooperative, rewarding and attentive behavior."

Goal: Turning a walk with your dog into a pleasurable stroll instead of a battle of wills between opposite ends of the leash.

The right equipment transforms tug-of-war dynamics into pleasurable strolls.

Loose-Leash Walking Steps

1. Indoors: Wearing the proper equipment (e.g., collar, head halter, no-pull harness or martingale collar), lure the dog to your right or left side. Command "SIT" and "LOOK-AT-ME" to gain his focus.

   Note: If the dog is on your left side, hold the leash in your right hand, leaving your left hand free as your TOUCH TARGET/treat dispenser hand. (Reverse this if dog is on your right side.)

2. Take a few steps forward at a normal pace while keeping your TOUCH TARGET palm facing backward and down by your side. This signals a dog to stay near your side. As soon as he is walking next to you, mark "YES" and treat. Continue walking and showing him your treat-filled TOUCH TARGET hand every four or five steps. Keep a loose leash and continue this pattern by repeating this "dress rehearsal" in other rooms of your house.

3. Advance the "dress rehearsal" to the foyer, lobby or mudroom area. Using a TOUCH TARGET hand practice walking slowly, with steady steps and the dog at your side. When he's reliably paying attention inside, it's time to take him outdoors.

4. Outdoors: Find a street or area with the fewest distractions and repeat steps 1–3. It's helpful to keep a treat behind your thumb as an alluring treat dispenser. Add an occasional LOOK-AT-ME along with a TOUCH TARGET command every few steps while reinforcing with praise and treats.

Strategies for the Noncompliant Dog

1. Whenever he pulls, stop immediately and wait for him to look back at you. Once that happens, lure him back to your side with a treat

and resume walking. You may need to repeat this action several times as this step requires patience.

2. Moving forward without pulling is the behavior you want to reinforce. Be consistent about stopping every time he pulls. Eventually, he'll get the idea that moving happens on cue and only when he is by your side.

3. Another tactic for pullers is to quickly turn and go in the opposite direction. It's called an about-face turn and it forces him to follow you. When he catches up to you, keep walking and lure him with TOUCH TARGET, then mark "YES" and treat. For the more challenging or stubborn dog, this will need to be repeated several times. This step also requires patience, timing and coordination.

4. For a lollygagger or leash dragger, place a squeaky toy or ball in your pocket. If he's showing no interest in walking, engage his prey drive by showing him a toy or by tossing him a toy ahead of you. As he starts moving toward the toy or ball, mark "YES" and treat. Engage his interest and motivate him to pick up his pace.

Note: High-energy "party animal" dogs may require a faster pace to keep their attention. More relaxed, senior or sensitive-poet dogs might require an unhurried, casual stride. Once a dog is reliable with his position next to you, add "HEEL" or "GOOD WALK" when the leash is in an L shape.

SWAGGER DIARIES: FLUFFY MOVES LIKE JAGGER

Like people, dogs have different walking styles. Challenging gaits for the loose-leash walker are:

Zigzag Walker: These dogs, without the aid of alcohol, would still fail a sobriety test.

Solution: When he crosses lanes, come to a complete STOP and give him no attention. Be prepared to pepper the walk with loads of LOOK-AT-ME and TOUCH TARGET commands. These impulse-challenged pooches are not above the law of loose-leash walking.

Urban Protester: Dogs that stop dead in their tracks. Bulldogs and puppies tend to fall into this category, but toy dogs are the poster pups for this label since you often see them in their owners' arms or in their own designer pooch bags.

Solution: Learn-to-earn is the way to motivate a dog that goes on strike. "No walk = no eat" turns a canine activist into a loose-leash advocate.

Pee-Many or Sniff-aholic: If you sniff or pee on everything, does it legally make it yours? Many dog owners attest that, if peeing or sniffing equaled ownership, their dogs would be real estate tycoons.

Solution: Once a dog has relieved himself and has had the opportunity to be a dog, it's time to engage him in something more rewarding, e.g., his favorite toy. As his leg starts to lift, squeak the toy and keep walking. He'll follow willingly after his prized toy. The target stick might also be something to gain his attention while walking.

Tourist Walker: These dogs stop repeatedly to investigate a new sight, sound, smell or object. Urbanites compare them to out-of-town "parade watchers," whom you hate walking behind because they're slow and get in the way of fast-moving city folks.

Solution: These pooches may require patience because they have less stamina or an ultra-relaxed canine-ality. Life can sometimes speed by with little meaning. Enjoy the slow strolls with a pooch that enjoys and treasures your companionship.

Pomo's trademark walk styles, not suited for
every owner, are endearing to his.

LEAD THE WAY

Not all owners object to the leash reactivity of their dogs. Pomo, a nine-year-old shih tzu, embodies each of the walk styles in this chapter. He's a zigzagger, a tourist walker, an urban protester, a pee-many and a sniff-aholic. His owners know to add an extra twenty minutes onto his four or five daily walks. Tony, his owner, shared: "While Pomo is challenging to walk, he's just the greatest dog in all the ways that matter most to us. He's a CEO outdoors, but indoors he's a real team player. He's never been a scavenger, he's social with other dogs and people and he's an experienced traveler. We've taken him all over the U.S., even to France. He loves his walks—his way. Kate suggested a no-pull harness for Pomo, but he resisted it, or maybe I did. I tolerate his crazy walks because I enjoy him so much and he makes me laugh—and sometimes he leads me to more interesting places in life."

If Pomo were an aggressive dog, this behavior would not be acceptable. Otherwise, it's up to the owner to decide what is acceptable and tolerable. The purpose of training is to adjust a dog's behavior to best suit an owner's lifestyle while ensuring all aspects of the dog's welfare. It's never meant to strip a dog of his unique traits. Cooperation dog training seeks to modify unwelcome, noncompliant canine behavior that poses a lifestyle or safety risk.

TRAINING TECHNIQUES SPECIFIC TO MAYBELLINE

When leash issues arise, emotions at both ends of the leash can become heightened. Owners and dogs in this situation need to rebuild their confidence and connection with one another. Toni, a professional tap-dance teacher, had all the right moves. Maybelline, a party girl cutie, had the capability to be responsive. They needed to develop a trust in each other while giving the equipment an adjustment period.

Two years without any training and a lack of socialization had left Maybelline an "awkward beauty."

Training Solution: It was best for Maybelline to avoid other dogs until she was familiar with the new equipment and reliable with Pay Attention commands.

MODIFIED TIE DOWN: Her excitement at meeting other dogs was overwhelming and needed to be restrained, but not by pulling. If it got to that level and LOOK-AT-ME failed, the next step was a TIE DOWN, i.e., Toni stepping on the leash. A TIE DOWN is a temporary management technique that takes away the two-way opposition reflex between owner and dog while neutralizing the emotions.

MODIFIED TIE DOWNS act as calming aids that ground the energy at both ends of the leash. They effectively stop the tug-of-war intensity by removing owner opposition from the situation. Maybelline would stop her lunging behavior because no energy would be feeding into it. As soon as she was calm, that behavior was rewarded and reinforced with praise and treats. The SIT command was also added to increase management and to further redirect her focus (counterconditioning).

DANCING WITH MY DOG

"Kate encouraged me to have fun with the training. She'd say, 'You can do it. You're a dancer—move and connect with your partner.' I listened and applied myself more freely to the process. I started to see training not as a job, but as a means of developing a relationship with Maybelline. The leash became less about having equipment and more about the commitment to each other. I also began taking time to play with her and discovered that she was a very serious player who was highly motivated to chase balls. My tone of voice took on more excitement and that revealed another means of getting her 'on-leash' attention. We were mixing it up more on life's dance floor. Maybelline started tuning in to me because I was less serious and more fun to be around. The no-pull harness pulled us together."

Good leash behavior should:

1. Secure safety for you and your dog.
2. Establish an owner as an inspired leader.
3. Enable you to enjoy walks with your dog.

Let It Play Out

P lay is an invaluable training tool at every stage of a dog's life. It's a rewarding and interactive management tool for owners. Play draws them to us and is often why we got a dog in the first place. An important part of ownership is having fun with your dog every day. There doesn't have to be a reason for playing, but I remind owners that the moment they initiate play with their dog, there is an opportunity to train. Playtime can be filled with techniques that teach a dog (1) self-control, (2) social intelligence and (3) confidence.

Play training demonstrates that a dog complies with commands because he wants to and not because an owner is dominant over him. Desired responses are increased when training is linked with the canine motivational drive of having fun. I use it as a motivating technique to channel "unwanted" behaviors into cued and purposeful ones.

Owners who stop training their dogs after completing obedience classes may find unwanted or destructive behavior cropping up. That doesn't mean that the dogs have forgotten everything they learned or become bad. Dogs that aren't provided with enough exercise or mental stimulation will resort to making up their own "bored-games." If that happens to your dog, don't get upset. Instead analyze his behavior to glean insight into the underpinnings of his drives, canine-ality and learning style. Incorporate a Sherlock Canine Holmes strategy and, more importantly, seek to find avenues that bring out the more lighthearted side of your dog.

When observing your dog, which of the following instinctive play styles do you see?

1. He prefers physical games like RETRIEVE and games involving agility.
2. He likes the mental challenge of a SEARCH AND RESCUE operation.
3. He's a performer that leans toward tricks, such as GIVE ME PAW, SNEEZE, SPEAK.
4. He likes to dance (canine freestyle).
5. Another style?

CHARLIE

Charlie is a pure party animal with an imaginary lamp shade mischievously perched on his head. He's Jimmy Fallon in a Havanese costume and can't keep a straight face when he looks at you. He has spot-on comedic timing and a strong work ethic. His sweet, agreeable disposition and people-pleasing pack drive are enhanced by his *"What's next?"* learning style. Carol and Bob, Charlie's owners, successfully tackled his puppyhood issues, basic obedience training and tailgating needs. They were consistent and compliant with the cooperation training methods. The

Charlie's owners sought training techniques that were
playful for both ends of the leash.

"What's next?" learning style in this family wasn't exclusive to Charlie. Carol, also a party animal type, has the *"What's next?"* drive. She also connected to the heart of training: having fun and just laughing. Their favorite games involve partnered activities where Carol choreographs Charlie dancing on his back legs or has him performing HIGH-FIVES with her.

> Play strengthens the bond between owners and dogs. It also provides physical exercise and mental stimulation for both ends of the leash.

INSTINCTUAL MATTERS

Dogs can easily be taught to redirect their instinctive behavior into acceptable play behavior. Their natural talents (behaviors) can be put on cue commands. They love figuring things out and performing and they enjoy the attention. Normal, though unwanted, "dog" behaviors (e.g., digging and barking) still need to be expressed, but they can be modified, managed and turned into playtime activities. Play gives dogs the opportunity to adapt their instinctive and cultivated abilities (drives), which they once depended on as a means of survival, into performance-worthy skills and tricks. And it still lets a dog be a dog.

Below is a chart of common undesirable behaviors that can be shaped into acceptable and managed ones.

Instinctual Behavior	Modified Play
Barking	SPEAK—owner cues behavior on and off. Instead of barking whenever the dog wants to, turn it into a trick. A great trick for the excessive barker in the family—every time the dog barks, mark "YES" and treat; as soon as he stops, command "QUIET" and treat.
Digging	FIND THE TOY—fill a basket with toys, placing the dog's favorite at the bottom where he'll have to dig it out. Or place a treat under a towel or beneath a dog's bed so he'll have to dig it out.
Fighting	TUG-OF-WAR—owner-initiated activity that allows a dog to tussle and wrestle within acceptable limits. Adherence to the STOP and DROP IT command must be immediate. Pauses during play reinforce good canine impulse control.
Herding	HIDE & SEEK—put a dog in SIT or DOWN and command STAY, then secure a hiding place and command, FIND ME. Be sure to toss in a few JOLLY EFFECT peekaboo looks to entice him to seek you out. (Certain breeds have an inherent drive for herding tasks like rounding up family members.)

Hunting	GO FIND IT—this activity trains and conditions dogs that are professional outdoor scavengers to take sniff cues from their owners. The more rewarding GO FIND IT becomes for a dog indoors, the more he learns to pay attention to the owner outdoors. It's a way for an owner to turn a particular drive on and off.

PLAY BENEFITS

Play training develops conditioned or associated responses that get a dog to think and strategize. It also builds canine character, which comes from learning consequences. Games last longer when a dog keeps his impulse behavior in check. If he doesn't, he risks losing out on playtime.

Below are two examples of play benefits. They include bonding, exercise, mental stimulation and increased canine impulse control:

- Owner-initiated tug-of-war games keep a dog aware of controlling his mouth (bite inhibition training). If he bites or becomes too mouthy, the game ends and he loses out on an activity he enjoys. Alert and cooperative behavior is rewarded.

  Fido's Take: *"Command cues such as STOP and DROP IT must be immediately responded to or else playtime ends. Chewing is for bones and certain toys. Follow the rules and game on!"*

- The command sequence "SPIN, SIT and DOWN" can be taught to exuberant canine greeters that jump on guests. Apply a cue word such as "SAY HELLO" to this chain of commands and guests will view Spot's SAY HELLO welcome as charming, not bothersome, behavior. He will earn more socializing opportunities while his owners receive compliments. It's a win-win dynamic with all parties set up for success and a fabulous time.

Spot's Take: *"My owners used to put me in my crate whenever visitors came over. Now they brush me and tell me that people are coming. It gets me so excited that sometimes I SAY HELLO without being cued* [anticipatory canine behavior]. *That cracks my owners up and earns me praise."*

Play is also terrific for creating a distraction to gain focus. It can be used to override fear of another dog, a thunderstorm or the vet's office. It's a quick way of changing a dog's mind-set and engaging him in another activity. If in a given circumstance a dog is too distracted or anxious to play, it's important to note such behavior, which tells an owner that the dog's threshold of tolerance is being challenged. This reactivity should not be ignored. A stressed dog will not play. Identify what's triggering the behavior and work on desensitization and counterconditioning techniques with him.

NIFTY TRAINING TOOLS

Games and play are built on structure and rules that encourage canine manners and provide boundaries for pushy pooches. These types learn that canine play is accompanied by a SIMON SAYS policy whereby owners eliminate players that don't follow instructions. Dogs, even the pushy ones, don't want to be benched in a game. They quickly rethink their actions and even become more patient.

The following training tools can be disguised as games and activities:

- CHASE
- DIG
- DROP IT
- FIND IT

- FETCH
- FREEZE
- GIVE ME PAW
- GO TO YOUR BED
- HIDE & SEEK
- HIGH-FIVE
- LEAVE IT
- ROLL OVER
- DANCE
- SHAKE
- SNEEZE
- SPEAK
- SPIN
- TUG-OF-WAR
- JUMP OVER
- CRAWL UNDER

PLAY VIBE

Cooperation dog training is best taught in a relaxed and playful atmosphere. Play is a primary and innovative means of motivating and reinforcing canine cooperative and compliant behavior. The more fun you make the training process for your dog, the easier it is to reduce challenges and find mutual interests. This is especially useful once you have passed the training benchmarks and want your dog to continue learning. Play also reduces stress, fear and aggression in both people and dogs.

TUCKER FACTOR

The SPIN command turned out to be useful, playful and therapeutic for Tucker.

Introducing fun into the training process often creates a catalyst that sparks owners to become more innovative in connecting with their dogs. Dogs pick up on this relaxed energy and respond to it positively. Training sessions turn into playful interactions that reinforce trust at both ends of the leash. Innovative owners like Caryl and Gary, discussed in an earlier chapter, have developed unique play sequences to counter Tucker's reactivity and extreme sensitivity to touch. For example, to clean his feet after a snowstorm, a performance is staged in which their Jack Russell does spins and rollovers and delights in being on his back while Caryl or Gary cleans off his dirty feet with a warm towel.

Through the joy of playing, Tucker gained trust and confidence in his owners. The frolicking, cued commands took him to a different state of mind that's incompatible with aggression. He gets carried away in a pleasurable, fired-up state like anyone who plays his heart out. Now Caryl and Gary's problem is coming up with more creative ideas for their canine genius. The very act of play sets up expectations of his behavior anytime and anywhere. "Play-training was a turning point for us. It changed Tucker from 'I can't do this' to 'I really love to do this stuff.' He's no ordinary dog. He's extraordinary," said Tucker's owners.

FEATURED TRAINING
TECHNIQUE: SPIN

Quick Description: SPIN

SPIN is a command that teaches a dog to go around in left or right circles.

- For high-energy dogs with a party animal canine-ality, SPIN is fun to do and provides additional exercise and mental stimulation.
- If a dog has dirty or wet feet, SPIN performed on top of a towel helps with the cleanup.
- It's a good trick command that trainers of all ages can easily teach a dog.
- For touch-sensitive dogs like Tucker, SPIN is a building block command that establishes trust and develops cooperative behavior.

Goal: SPIN is about having fun.

1. Place a high-value treat or favorite toy in front of the dog's nose and move it around to the side of the dog's body in a slow and exaggerated circular movement. It will be instinctual for him to follow the lure with his head and nose, with body following.
2. As he completes the circular movement mark "YES" and treat. Repeat five to ten times. Be sure to toss in one or two JACKPOT REWARDS to maintain the dog's interest.

   Note: Some dogs need additional motivation to complete the full turn. Use the shaping tool strategy and mark "YES" with a treat at the halfway point of the turn. Continue to coax (and shape) until he completes a SPIN. Be sure to add extra-yummy treats to keep his interest as you extend the halfway point with an exaggerated lure. Do this until he completes a SPIN, earning a JACKPOT RE-WARD and praise.

3. Once the dog is spinning reliably, gradually refine the exaggerated luring motion to being just your index finger circling over his head as you come into a standing position.

4. When the dog consistently spins 360 degrees with the index finger cue, add the command "SPIN." Mark "YES" after the completed SPIN. Praise and treat. Repeat five to ten times, adding in a few JACKPOT REWARDS for faster responses.

5. Increase the dog's versatility and add to the fun factor by practicing SPIN RIGHT and SPIN LEFT. Multiple SPINs interspersed with SIT and ROLL OVER can also be added to create canine calisthenics for a rainy day.

6. If the dog stops at any point, go back to the level where he had success and rework shaping and capturing the desired behavior.

Note: If you're thinking of advancing to a trick class, or planning on doing agility work, SPIN can be achieved with a TARGET STICK (a retractable stick). Replace the circular hand gesture with a TARGET STICK in the training steps listed above. The advantage of using a TARGET STICK for tricks and agility work is that it's user-friendly. It also will likely speed up teaching a dog to go through tunnels, jump over bars and weave around cones.

CANINE UNIVERSITY

Watching puppies play at four to six weeks of age can be a captivating experience. They pounce, chase, mouth and barrel into one another over and over again. It can look like the furry version of World Wrestling Entertainment. Each pup takes his turn convincing another of his feigned ferociousness. There's an artful and instructional Jekyll and Hyde role-playing that takes place. Every once in a while, the "play" escalates and one pup goes too far with biting or roughhousing. In response, the other pup yelps, thereby letting the sibling know *"That hurt. Don't do that again or I won't play with you anymore."* That high-pitched squeal imparts a lesson about bite inhibition and helps establish an understanding of cooperative social interactions and acceptable communal behavior.

Puppies want other puppies to keep playing with them. Give-and-take dynamics serve as the rules of the game. Puppies that fail to modify their conduct when told *"You bite too hard"* or *"You play too rough"* will find out that not playing by the rules ends the game. Replicating aspects of the canine whelping-pen university is an ideal way to foster cooperative learning. Play, the foundation of puppyhood, and heart of cooperative learning, imparts many important principles of training, such as reinforcement, teamwork, building trust and meeting expectations. It reduces owners' stress and turns them into circus ringleaders rather than drill sergeants.

PAUSE AND PLAY REALITIES

The challenge of dog play is that many owners are not sure how to distinguish play (normal behavior) from aggression. At its peak, dog play duplicates many behavioral traits that, in a different context or circumstance, could be offensive, dangerous or generally unacceptable to owners (e.g., growling, mouthing, tussling or mock-pummeling). However, in dog play, what's exhibited is exaggerated behavior that involves cooperation. Taking turns and sequenced movements of semi-orchestrated actions are their version of "Cowboys and Indians" or "Cops and Robbers." Eyeing, stalking, chasing, catching, tagging and tumbling are pooch playground games.

The heightened energy level must remain controlled and tolerable for each player. There's a farcical fluidity with playful canine behavior that reads as nonthreatening. A "play face," a wide-open, relaxed mouth with tongue hanging to the side, may also be recognizable. The dog's soft gaze and goofy grin will likely resemble those of famous cartoon dogs.

Pausing between stalking, pawing and barking adds to the *"Gotcha,"* a teasing enticement among dogs. Those pauses also represent a regrouping and polite signaling (reminder) to each other that this is play and not behavior intended to escalate into fighting. The pauses are thumbs-up signs signaling, *"We're good, right?"* or *"Let's take a break."* They can vary, be staggered or appear between bursts of energy. Sometimes they are dramatic, sometimes subtle, but they should happen frequently while two or more dogs are playing. They indicate a sense of impulse control. Taking actions such as wrestling or mock fighting too far will end the game and ruin a good time. Identifying when a dog crosses the line toward aggression can be challenging for owners. Look for play pauses, which indicate that your dog is operating on a sophisticated level of self-control.

APPROPRIATE VERSUS INAPPROPRIATE PLAY

APPROPRIATE PLAY SIGNS	INAPPROPRIATE PLAY SIGNS
Play bows are invitational gestures that communicate: *"Wanna play?"* Think of them as canine peace signs.	Incessant barking while interacting with another dog. An in-your-muzzle (face) combative energy.

Play sneezes are less *"Achoo"* and more *"Hiya, hiya, hiya, and howdy— whaddaya say we play?"* expressions of a dog's excitement.	"Bully-tackling" amounts to pummeling another dog. It can include body slams and pinning a dog against a surface. The more vulnerable dog may exhibit signs of fear (i.e., tucked tail or yelping), and the situation could escalate to a fight.
Hip checks are a way people are playful with one another on and off the dance floor. Pooches carry on the hip-check *"gotcha"* tease, adding a turning-away move for an extra edge.	Not getting off a dog once he's pinned down, especially if the other dog is squealing. Simply put: unrestrained bullying tactic.
Pausing between heightened states of activity allows for an ongoing contest called "Who can make the goofiest dog grin?"	Not pausing between play. Canine play pauses should happen frequently for both dogs to maintain emotional control. They serve as reminders that interactions have playful intentions, not aggressive ones.
Taking turns. One dog is not overly dominant. Each has to show off his versatility.	Biting hard on and shaking the neck of another dog.

INTERVENTION TIME

Canine body language that suddenly turns from relaxed to tense (stiff and freezing) indicates that a dog's threshold of tolerance is being challenged. Dogs may begin to circle one another with cautionary steps that indicate a potential "face-off" conflict. It's important for owners to read canine visual discourse and to intervene when play turns into disagreement. If this happens, create a distraction to change the dog's mind-set and reestablish his focus. Try one or more of the following:

- Interrupt with the sound "EH-EH"
- Squeak a toy
- Command "COME" or "LEAVE IT"
- Snap on the leash and leave

A short-and-sweet approach to training and playing is a very important strategy. The biggest challenge at dog parks stems from owners not realizing they have to keep an eye on their dogs. Would you take your eyes off a five-year-old in a playground? Or become so engaged in conversation with another parent that you lose track of where your child is? Dogs need supervision in those situations. Safety between dogs and the public must be an owner priority. Avoid treating the dog run like you're at Starbucks with a friend. Instead, view it as a Sherlock Canine Holmes opportunity to gain more insight into your dog's play style.

THERE'S A NEW SHERIFF IN TOWN

Sophie, my pug, is the sheriff of puppy socialization classes. Once the puppies are acclimated to the environment and have had a chance to ad-

Sheriff Sophie teaches pups canine manners.

just, I unleash her to make the rounds. She's the older bitch that pups defer to at her "backing off" cues when playing gets too rough. Her cut-off signals inform a pup that his curious sniffing or playing has reached unacceptable levels. Puppies are also welcome to play-challenge with her as she, too, enjoys the interactions.

Nevertheless, if you challenge Sophie's authority, expect to be put in your place. No harm will come to a pup, but a reprimand will be given in the form of a bark-bark Sophie lecture: *"Did you see me lick my lips? Turn my head? How about when I turned and went in the other direction? Knucklehead—those are all signals. I was talking to you! I like your chutz-pah and it's okay to challenge, but it's also very important to know when to back off. That's all I'm saying. Now don't get wimpy on me. Next time just pause and let me know you hear me. Maybe put yourself in a time-out. Now get up and shake off—show me there's no hard feelings, little fellow."*

LET IT PLAY OUT

When owners come to my puppy socialization classes, I take them through the basic steps. First challenges and issues are discussed in round-robin fashion to tailor the class to specific needs. Next we work on commands such as LOOK-AT-ME and TOUCH TARGET. After thirty minutes, owners and dogs are more at ease and ready for the final lesson. I then announce that it's time for leashes to be unhooked and for pups to interact.

Sophie begins to roam among the puppies to monitor behavior and discipline. While this is taking place, I narrate the canine interactions:

> "Sky [Shorkie] and Oliver [dachshund] are showing really good play behavior. See how Oliver took a moment to pause before going back to wrestling with Sky? That 'play and pause' behavioral tempo is how dogs manage heightened arousal levels and avoid fights. The pause is used to regroup and to check in with playmates. What they're saying is: *'Everything is cool, right? You know we're just playing, not fighting?'* Sky is wagging her tail and responding with a 'thumbs-up' play bow to encourage Oliver to continue play fighting with her."

When two pups tussle and a nervous owner wants to step in, I'll say, "Let it play out." I know the difference between playing and fighting. I provide owners with an observational course that helps them identify give-and-take maneuvers and the role reversal of two pups.

> "Sky is no longer the one being pursued. They've switched roles. She's now chasing after Oliver. That's give-and-take canine play behavior. Notice that both of their faces are relaxed. Their goofy expressions indicate that neither is fearful. Their body slamming, tackles and chasing are normal, healthy play behaviors."

Owners need to gain the confidence to "let it play out" in a supervised setting. Sophie, not the owners, will step in when needed. Some dogs are more vocal players, while others need to learn to take breaks in their play (pauses). Every dog has an individual play style. A stronger dog may need to curb his enthusiasm because if he plays too rough he'll be either ignored or corrected. And of course Sophie will dash over if the little fellow gets carried away.

The key is to understand when you should let it play out and when it's gone too far. For over ten years, Sophie has gracefully given owners the necessary insight to gauge the difference between desirable and undesirable play behavior. Dogs learn from one another. They need to be with their own kind and to speak among themselves in their native tongue. Playing is teaching.

A dog yelping during play is a submissive distress call that might indicate fear, pain or frustration. It can be saying to another pup, *"Back off."* An owner should hear a yelp as "help" but within the context.

DISTANCE AND DURATION TRAINING

Play activities, such as FETCH, HIDE & SEEK and CHASE, are a good way to train for distance and duration. All of these games can be played with the dog close by and then be advanced to greater distances. The duration of an activity will depend on how long reliable and cooperative behavior lasts. Keeping all training sessions short, sweet and rewarding is the best way to produce positive results.

SMART PLAY

When the owners of Lilly, a Chihuahua, discovered that their dog had gone into a closet and pulled all their laundry into a corner of the bedroom, I told them they have a smart dog. She's capable of doing more with her basic education. Lilly is letting them know she's bored and not getting enough exercise or mental stimulation.

Lilly's ingenious way of occupying her time is not pleasing to her owners. However, with a little modification and tweaking, let's look at what can happen.

Lilly Tidies Up:

1. Set the stage with an empty toy bin and several toys ready to be placed in it.
2. Take the dog's favorite toy and hold it over the bin. Let her take it from you, then quickly command "DROP IT" so that it falls into the bin. Praise and treat her. Repeat five to ten times.
3. Using playful energy, take the same toy and toss it a short distance away. Command "FETCH" and give the dog a chance to grab the toy before cueing "COME." As she runs over and nears the toy box, command "DROP IT," then praise and treat. Repeat five to ten times.
4. Take a new toy and, with playful energy, repeat steps 1–3. Putting toys away will be turned into a rewarding action game that the dog enjoys playing over and over again.
5. Once "FETCH-COME-DROP IT" becomes a sequence of reliable behavior, start to link the commands into one cue: TIDY UP. Be energetic, upbeat and quick with your timing.

> Play training is a continuing education course that advances the basic skills of SIT, DOWN, STAY and COME and converts them into games and tricks.

TRAINING TECHNIQUES SPECIFIC TO CHARLIE

"Bob and I made a decision to do everything different with Charlie, our Havenese," said Carol. "Phoebe, our previous dog, had been very sick and couldn't do a lot of stuff. Playing with other dogs was off limits because normal dog antics like pawing, body slamming and mounting could cause her to bleed internally. We had been everything to her—both guardians and playmates."

Bob and Carol had both been looking to add a playful pooch to their household and were seeking a fun approach to training. We'd work on SIT and Charlie would perform in a way that said, *"Wanna see what else I can do? I mean, SIT is very rudimentary."*

Carol picked up on her dog's enthusiasm, adding, "What else do you think he can do?" Which led to his first trick of spinning while dancing on two hind legs. That earned a "Bob! Get in here quick—you won't believe what Charlie just learned!"

Charlie leaps over a record number of designer bags seeking
to earn a place in the pages of *Guinness World Records*.

The focus of the next session was the DOWN/STAY command. Once accomplished, both Carol and Charlie turned and looked at me, Carol in wonder and Charlie's expression eager for more. So I quickly asked Carol to help me line up her handbag and Charlie's Sherpa bag. Using a target stick and a TOUCH TARGET hand signal, I cued Charlie to JUMP. He flew over the bags, earning a "Bob! Get in here quick—you won't believe what Charlie just learned!"

STAY and LEAVE IT lessons also included more tricks that taught Charlie to turn light switches on and off on cue and ring a bell to go outside. And, yes, they earned another "Bob!" The COME command brought out Carol's sense of humor. She decided to line up several of her handbags to create an Evel Canine-Knievel Yves Saint Laurent bag jump, earning another "Bob!"

Carol and Bob are special owners. Every time Carol called her husband, he entered the room, observed, nodded and said, "I knew Charlie was smart." Then he exited, only to return a few minutes later. Carol's "Bob!" often pops into my mind and makes me laugh. It's the feeling I want for all my clients. Training is not about competition or doing something correctly or incorrectly. It's simply about finding a unique and fun-filled training path for both ends of the leash.

PLAY STYLES

Genetics, early socialization and environment all impact and shape a dog's play style. Certain breeds, such as herding dogs, are more inclined toward running and chasing. Terriers may bring a feisty, high-energy conviction to their interactions with other dogs and people. Working dogs like German shepherds, with their predisposition to protect and guard, often exhibit a "bark-bark" vocalization and bring a cornering style of frolicking to play. Golden retrievers, of the sporting breed, might settle in

Ollie keeps careful watch to make sure Desmond plays by the rules.

for team-oriented play that includes parallel running and Frisbee and ball chasing. The point is that various breed-specific traits will likely influence a dog's play style.

Dogs have individual play styles and they gravitate, like we would, to others who share their interests and play habits. However, dogs' play is built around their instincts for fighting, predation, role reversal, chase and other variations and combinations of these activities. Expect body slamming, hip checks, mouthing, jumping, wrestling and darting. Two dogs may pin each other to the ground, release and then do it all over again. What you'll notice in dog runs is that, often over breed, age or size, dogs tend to seek partners with comparable and compatible play styles.

Let's look at the play styles of several dogs in this book:

- **Tucker** (owners Caryl and Gary—chapter 3): "Tom Brady mentality" where he commits to memory every call (command) that owners craft in their personalized trainer playbook. **Tucker**: *"I want to be perfect. I want to win championships."*
  Play details: Tucker loves the sequenced commands SPIN, DOWN, ROLL OVER, FETCH and many more! He also adores

playing with interactive pet activity toys and treat puzzles designed by Nina Ottosson where he has to slide open lots of different compartments to find treats.

- **Ollie** (owners Desmond and Andrew—chapter 4): "Kentucky Derby qualifier" that jogs every day with Desmond and is determined to pass runners with ponytails. Like Mine That Bird, the 2009 Derby winner, he's a come-from-behind type that goes up on the rail and shoots Desmond a *"Time to pass"* glance before threading himself into the lead.

  Desmond: "I can't help but laugh at how intent he is on accomplishing his goal. As soon as we are far enough ahead, he looks back and then up at me with a grin as if to say, *'How cool was that!'* I can't argue since he brings out the competitor in me."

  Play Details: Herding, herding and herding have been redirected to interactive intelligence games that exercise another facet of his canine-ality. Ollie earns treats and IQ points by pulling, lifting, pushing, sliding and manipulating the blocks and knobs in his board games.

- **Sophie** (my dog!—chapter 9): Sophie's play style is professorial. She plans everything. Her routine is meticulous and her approach to play is orderly. If thinking were to become an Olympic sport, she'd be wearing a gold medal on her collar. At home she lets go and runs about wagging her tail. Sometimes I feel the need to check her bowl to make sure that what she's drinking is water, not a cocktail.

  Play Details: She loves to practice her spins. Like Tucker, she wipes her feet in spin fashion, earning a towel tug-of-war for good measure. She's also always up for a good game of HIDE & SEEK.

- **Charlie** (owners Carol and Bob—chapter 12): "Feedback Applause" style describes this Havanese that loves to wow the crowd and earn Carol's Lucille Ball impersonation: "Bob! Get in here quick—you won't believe what Charlie just learned!"

Play Details: Charlie creates his own games, including the "knickers-slingshot." This game came about when Charlie engineered undergarments hanging on a doorknob into a slingshot. The first time knickers were presented to Carol she assumed they had fallen off the handle. Carol returned them to the handle only to have Charlie hand them back to her for a reload. FYI: Charlie is also an excessive celebrator. After completing a trick, he'll top it off by dancing on his hind legs for additional applause.

BECOME THE BEST TRAINER FOR YOUR DOG

The best part of my job is getting you to see the world through your dog's eyes. The slightest head movement, flicker of ears or licking of lips is his way of communicating with you. His bark tells you one thing, his tail swing informs you of something else and his positioning and stance is yet another bit of information that needs translating. The true nature of our dogs is complex and intriguing. In humanizing our pets, we often forget about their instincts and drives—their way of being in the world. It's different from ours. I've gotten inside the minds of dogs and understand their point of view.

I've come to appreciate what our dogs can teach us. As a dog trainer, my goal is to build the bond between you and your dog in fun and innovative ways that are aligned and designed for both ends of the leash. I'm here to help you recognize your dog's traits and provide you with the training tools to modify and shape his behavior. My job is to coach you to become the best trainer for your dog.

COOPERATION TRAINING GRADUATES

ACKNOWLEDGMENTS

When working on a project of this scope, it cannot be done without the help, love and support of ALL the people in your life along the way. With deep appreciation to everyone and every lesson I had to learn before this project began and throughout the last two years.

To my mother, my first mentor for teaching me how to care for and respect animals and especially to not over-humanize. A true gift, thank you!

To my wonderful five sisters, who have been so supportive throughout my life, and especially during the last two years with my first book!!

To Bruce Weber and Nan Bush, for trusting and giving me the opportunity to care for their pack of amazing dogs. These beautiful dogs taught me so much about the dynamics of a pack living, an invaluable lesson for me as a trainer.

Thanks to all their staff members for being so kind and supportive, especially Lisa Merkle. And for introducing me to Breon O'Farrell, dog trainer and mentor to me. You helped build my confidence as a trainer. Thank you!

To the late Jane Tiff, first owner to Sophie and who insisted I take Sophie when she became ill, when I was actually looking to rescue a Great Dane or mastiff.

To Sophie, my velvet black pug, the best dog trainer to the puppies! She has taught me so much about what it is to be a big personality dog in a little body.

To all the owners and dogs that for more than twelve years have given me the opportunity to work with them, I'm deeply appreciative; for without those experiences, it would not have been possible to write this book. Thank you!

To the owners and dogs featured in this book, my sincere gratitude to you for trusting in me. Your willingness to share your experiences for this book will forever help other owners and dogs near and far.

To Animal Behavioral College, for trusting me as a mentor-trainer to their students. Thank you!

To APDT, for their seminars that introduced me to other fabulous trainers and behaviorists such as Ian Dunbar, Jean Donaldson, Nicole Wilde, Wendy Volhard, Pia Silvani, Pat Miller and Karen Pryor.

To my loyal dog-training "family": Sherri Bohlig, Marc Elias, Helen Buttolph, Jamie Baldanza, Damien Diaz and Brenda Nieves—thank you!

To all of my friends here and overseas who have hung in there with me during this process, especially when I was not always available: Bara De Cabrol, Kathleen Carthy, Nanci Dator, James Brummel, Jonathan Perlroth, Lizette & Gloriela Colon, Jerry Weissman, Erik Lieblein, Leslie Altmark and Lisa & Mark Steinhauer.

Special mention to Amanda Good Hennessey, for her continued love and support throughout this process. You always keep me laughing.

To Candy Moss and Lisa Neilson, who where among the first who encouraged me to write a book on training. Thanks for helping plant the seed. To Eileen Schulock, for the continued support throughout this process and assisting with my newsletter. To Robert Valin, for setting up my website and always rooting for me.

To Sari Carel, for taking the photos. And to the owners who supplied their shots.

Forever thankful to Charlotte Druckman for writing me up in *New York* magazine, which consequently changed my life and made my phone ring off the hook!

To all the vets who continue to recommend me as a trainer. Dr. Dianne DeLorenzo at Abingdon Square Veterinary Clinic veterinary behaviorist Dr. E'Lise Christensen, Dr. Julia Harmon and Dr. Stephanie Liff. Everyone at Center for Veterinary Care, West Village Veterinary practice and Washington Square Animal Hospital.

With much appreciation to Cara Bedick, for seeking me out and for guiding us through the first round of edits.

To Marisa Vigilante, my second editor, for jumping in at the tail end and helping us navigate to the finish line with great insight and enthusiasm.

To the rest of the team at Avery, Megan Newman, Bill Shinker, Patrick Nolan, Lisa Johnson, Lindsay Gordon and Casey Maloney, who have been so supportive and encouraging.

To Lynn Johnston, for her guidance throughout this process and keeping things on track.

To Caryl Glaab, for his creative and artistic sensibilities that he generously provided on many of the photographs in the book. And who, with his partner, Gary, Tucker's owners, embrace the heart of cooperation dog training. Thank you!

To Tony and Pomo, for their patience and support.

To Yvonne Conza, for understanding my style of training and adding her own canine expertise and research skills. Thanks for capturing my voice and for keeping the passion and perseverance throughout this process.

And last, to my son, Blake, for his patience when I had to be at the computer night after night. You are my sunshine.

—K.P.

To Kate Perry, for trusting in my words.

To Tony, my husband, for believing in me from the very moment we met. His sense of humor and support on this project was immeasurable in every way.

To Pomo, my wise and lovable shih tzu, who leads our family to interesting places in life. The day you were placed in my arms was the best day of my life.

To Julian Kreeger, my compassionate friend and lawyer, who predictably orders salmon for dinner. You kept me focused on what was important and trusted that I'd deliver.

To Judge Judy Kreeger, a friend that has always been there for me. Shout out to Pomo's poodle girlfriend, Jasmine Kreeger.

To Alan Nevins, an agent with class and an appreciation for writers. Thank you for being responsive, charming and always available to me.

To Debra, Joe, Nick and Collin Morgan, Ann Tierney, Uncle Roger, Kitty and Joe Conza, Carol and Pat Pompeo, for all your support and care.

To Dr. Pamela Schwartz and her surgical team, Dr. Jennifer Chaitman and Dr. Mark Rosenberg, for giving exceptional care to Pomo.

To "Tequila Chic" Diane Mandel, Irma Botier, Dr. Dollbreaker, Liz Margolies, Amy Vecchio and countless others who helped me through challenges and joined me in celebrations. Your bedrock friendship and guidance has meant the world to me.

To Peter Max, for teaching me about perseverance and drive.

To Shep Gordon, for opening doors for me because he could and for sharing a fondness for Buffalo, New York.

To Wendy Diamond, for inviting me on a memorable road trip and for giving me the opportunity to write for her magazine.

To David Frei, Director of Communications for the Westminster Kennel Club, thanks for giving me the opportunity to cover stories for the Westminster Kennel Club and for introducing me to amazing owners and champion breeds. There truly is only one WKC.

To Catherine Texier and Darcey Steinke and all my writing teachers who mentored me. Thank you for embracing my quirks while helping me to refine my craft.

To Elizabeth Baum, who came to my rescue on many occasions, even at our lunch where Richard Gere showed up.

To Corinne Fazzolari-Leone, Cliff Fazzolari, Tami Bucco, Susan Porcaro Goings, Karon Cohen, Madeline Vaz, Lauri Ward and countless others, for being there and for keeping it real.

To the dogs of 1500 Ocean Drive in Miami Beach that own my heart in every way.

To the owners featured in this book. I'm honored to know all of you and have been so moved by the relationships you have developed with your dogs. You lead the way in responsible and caring canine guardianship.

To Caryl Glaab, a rock star of gigantic proportion. You showed a generosity and talent that was so appreciated.

To Marisa Vigilante, a fearless editor who embraced this project with heart and humor.

To Cara Bedick, for finding this project.

—Y.C.

RESOURCES

BOOKS

Understanding Dogs and Their Behavior

Aloff, Brenda. *Canine Body Language: A Photographic Guide Interpreting the Native Language of the Domestic Dog.* Wenatchee, WA: Dogwise Publishing, 2005.

Donaldson, Jean. *The Culture Clash: A Revolutionary New Way of Understanding the Relationship Between Humans and Domestic Dogs.* Berkeley, CA: James & Kenneth Publishers, 1996.

Grandin, Temple, and Catherine Johnson. *Animals in Translation: Using the Mysteries of Autism to Decode Animal Behavior.* Boston: Mariner Books, 2006.

Horowitz, Alexandra. *Inside of a Dog: What Dogs See, Smell, and Know.* New York: Scribner's, 2010.

Rugaas, Turid. *On Talking Terms with Dogs: Calming Signals*, second edition. Wenatchee, WA: Dogwise Publishing, 2005.

Wilde, Nicole, CPDT. *Help for Your Fearful Dog: A Step-by-Step Guide to Helping Your Dog Conquer His Fears*, first edition. Santa Clarita, CA: Phantom Publishing, 2006.

Puppy Stage

Dunbar, Dr. Ian. *After You Get Your Puppy.* Berkeley, CA: James & Kenneth Publishers, 2001.

———. *Before & After Getting Your Puppy: The Positive Approach to Raising a Happy, Healthy & Well-Behaved Dog.* Novato, CA: New World Library, 2004.

Child/Dog Relationship

Silvani, Pia, and Lynn Eckhardt. *Raising Puppies & Kids Together: A Guide for Parents.* Neptune City, NJ: TFH Publications, 2005.

Positive Reinforcement Dog Training

Dunbar, Dr. Ian. *How to Teach a New Dog Old Tricks*, third edition. Berkeley, CA: James & Kenneth Publishers, 1998.

Miller, Pat. *The Power of Positive Dog Training*. Hoboken, NJ: Howell Book House, 2001.

Pryor, Karen. *Don't Shoot the Dog! The New Art of Teaching and Training*, third edition. Lydney, Gloucestershire, UK: Ringpress Books, 2002.

Canine Behavior: Anxiety

McConnell, Patricia B., Ph.D. *The Cautious Canine: How to Help Dogs Conquer Their Fears*, second edition. Black Earth, WI: McConnell Publishing, 2005.

Wilde, Nicole, CPDT. *Don't Leave Me! Step-by-Step Help for Your Dog's Separation Anxiety*. Santa Clarita, CA: Phantom Publishing, 2010.

———. *Help for Your Fearful Dog: A Step-by-Step Guide to Helping Your Dog Conquer His Fears*. Santa Clarita, CA: Phantom Publishing, 2006.

Canine Health

Baxter, Roberta, MA, VetMB. *Mini Encyclopedia of Dog Health*. Consultant: Chris C. Pinney, DVM. Hauppauge, NY: Barron's Educational Series, 2011.

Brevitz, Betsy, DVM. *The Complete Healthy Dog Handbook: The Definitive Guide to Keeping Your Pet Happy, Healthy & Active*. New York: Workman Publishing, 2009.

Goldstein, Martin, DVM. *The Nature of Animal Healing: The Definitive Holistic Medicine Guide to Caring for Your Dog and Cat*. New York: Ballantine Books, 2000.

TRAINING AND TRICKS DVDS

The How of Bow Wow: Foundation Skills for All Dogs. www.takeabowwow.com.

Take a Bow Wow and *Bow Wow Take 2.* www. takeabowwow.com.

TRAINING RESOURCE ORGANIZATION

The Association of Pet Dog Trainers. www.APDT.com

DOG BEHAVIOR, HEALTH AND TRAINING: ONLINE READING RECOMMENDATIONS

ASPCA's Animal Poison Control Center. http://www.aspca.org/pet-care/poison-control/.

Spector, Dr. Donna. "Pet Food—What You Need to Know—for Your Pet's Sake." http://www.petmd.com/dog/nutrition/evr_pet_food_for_your_pets_sake#.T5d Yno5uHs0

www.dogwise.com
www.whole-dog-journal.com

PRODUCT RECOMMENDATIONS

Head Halter
Gentle Leader Headcollar by Premier Pets. www.premier.com.
Halti by the Company of Animals. www.companyofanimals.co.uk.

No-Pull Harness
Easy Walk Harness. www.premier.com.
Sensation No-Pull Harness or Easy Walk Harness. www.softouchconcepts.com.

Interactive Treat-Dispensing Dog Toys and Puzzles
Busy Buddy treat-dispensing toys. www.premier.com
Canine activity toys and puzzle games. www.nina-ottosson.com.

Apparel and Accessories: Grooming, Health, Crates, Gates, Playpen, Cleaning Supplies, Treats
www.eco-hound.com
www.petedge.com

PHOTO CREDITS

INDEX

ABOUT THE AUTHORS

Kate Perry grew up in the Canary Islands, Greece and England rescuing all kinds of animals. She moved to New York City in 1993 to pursue an acting career and then started her own dog walking business as a side job to help pay the bills. That quickly switched to her being a full-time dog trainer working alongside Breon O'Farrell. She apprenticed with him for two years, after which time she became partners with his training company for the following two years, as well as attending many dog training seminars run by APDT.com.

Kate is a member of the Association of Pet Dog Trainers (APDT) and is a certified dog trainer with the Animal Behavioral College, where she also works as a mentor-trainer teaching students how to become trainers in their own right. She has been training dogs for the last twelve years, and her philosophy and methodology center on the use of positive reinforcement. She was named Best Dog Trainer by *New York* magazine and has appeared on the *Weekend Today* show. Kate serves on the board of directors for the charity Rock & Rawhide, founded by Kylie Edmond and Sean-Patrick M. Hillman. She currently lives in Manhattan with her pug, Sophie, her cat, Jonny Pepper, and son, Blake.

Yvonne Conza, a writer and founder of the online site Woof Patrol (woofpatrol .com), has written and published more than one hundred articles for dog lovers. In 2006, she established a campaign titled *Winning Hearts, Minds and Tails,* which led to the changing of a Miami Beach law making it legal for dogs to stroll on the South Beach beach walk. Her stories and feature writings have appeared in *Animal Fair* magazine and the *Catskill Mountain Guide.* She also wrote two plays that were performed at the Off Center Theater and the Lee Strasberg Theatre and Film Institute in New York City. Yvonne is a former actress and a member of New York Women in Film and Television. She serves as a volunteer for the Boys and Girls Clubs of America.